Pathway to Music

FOR SUSAN

ANTONY HOPKINS
Pathway to Music

J. M. Dent & Sons Ltd
London & Melbourne

092683

First published 1983
© Text, Antony Hopkins

Printed in Great Britain by
Richard Clay (The Chaucer Press), Bungay, Suffolk
for J. M. Dent & Sons Ltd
Aldine House, 33 Welbeck Street, London W1M 8LX

This book is set in 11 on 13pt VIP Times
by D. P. Media Limited, Hitchin, Hertfordshire

British Library Cataloguing in Publication Data

Hopkins, Antony
  Pathway to music.
  1. Music
  I. Title
  780   ML160
ISBN 0-460-04580-6

Contents

Preface

Surely not *another* book on appreciating music, one is tempted to ask; hasn't the subject been covered extensively enough already? Well, of course there are numerous books, magazines, television and radio programmes, all designed to enhance the enjoyment of this, perhaps the most universal of all the arts. Indeed, it is a language of sorts, since Beethoven, Bach, Mozart or Stravinsky can 'speak' most eloquently to the members of virtually every nation without a word of explanation being uttered. But then to a certain and limited extent so can we all. We recognise tears, laughter, hunger, weariness, despair, hope or love in the expression of the human face, the carriage of the human body, the sound of the human voice, even though we may not comprehend the significance of the individual words uttered. A voice raised in anger conveys at least the gist of the matter although we may remain ignorant of its cause. A body drooping with fatigue tells us of its owner's state without recourse to conversation; eyes can express love, remorse, sorrow, compassion or hatred, even though scientists assure us that the eye itself can no more convey emotion than can a marble. This much is true also of music. In matters of emotion it is explicit, so much so that Mendelssohn found it less ambiguous than language:

> People often complain that music is too ambiguous; that what they should think when they hear it is so unclear, whereas everyone understands words. With me it is exactly the opposite, and not only with regard to an entire speech but also with individual words. These seem to me so ambiguous, so vague, so easily misunderstood in comparison to genuine music which fills the soul with a thousand things better than words. (*Letter to Marc-André Souchay, 15 October 1842.*)

It is a somewhat provocative view, more likely to come from a composer, to whom music is indeed an instinctive language, than from a listener, for whom it may well seem baffling at one moment and alluring at another. Yet when we think of alien languages we also think of interpreters, for while we may understand emotions such as I have already mentioned readily enough, the communication of *thought* is a different matter. We may in some distant land see a starving child; we can instantly recognise its distress, understand the significance of the outstretched hand, the tear-stained face, the swollen belly and the misshapen legs. There is no mistaking the message. But if the child starts to explain its plight in its native tongue – *'the soldiers came and took my father away and shot him; my mother is dying; our home was burnt down and I must travel many miles to find my uncle who perhaps may help us; meantime I have eaten nothing but roots and berries for five days; please help me'* – then, though the tone of voice will tell us something, the actual content will remain totally obscure. It is at such times that an interpreter is needed, and I regard it as no accident that we should use the same word to describe the function of the performing musician, he who interprets the music for us by bringing the printed page to life.

If we pursue the parallels between music and language, we find that the same holds true; emotions are easily recognisable, thoughts less so. But what, then, are musical thoughts; can a composer 'think' *in* music as opposed to thinking *about* it? When we think about any subject, familiar or obscure, we use words as the vehicle for thought, even though we may appear to be silent. Within the mind strings of words form; sometimes the vehicle comes to a halt; we are 'at a loss for a word'. Music, not all of it but certainly its major structures, might be described as a means of pursuing and developing a line of thought without the use of words. (The same might be said of mathematics although even numerical or algebraic symbols are identified with words; if I put down the number 1,257 on the page, your brain 'interprets' it not as an abstract but as one thousand two hundred and fifty-seven.)

Granted, then, that emotional music is easy to comprehend, it must also be accepted that cerebral music is a much harder proposition and that it may well need the services of an interpreter to clarify its meaning or purpose. Such has been my self-appointed task these past thirty years or more, for I am deeply aware that in an age when music is only too readily available at the flick of a switch, its currency may become devalued. Indeed, it is frequently forced upon us in places where it has no right to be, the supermarket, the railway station, the aircraft, even the dentist's. In exposing it to such unsympathetic environments we are demeaning it as an art, making it subservient to the prosaic needs of everyday existence when it properly deserves our respect and attention.

This book, in which I hope to serve as interpreter and guide, is designed to be not just a pathway to music, which suggests a finite journey at whose termination we arrive in much the same state as we were before we set out, but rather a journey of discovery into the heart of music itself. My aim is illumination, not anatomy, for the language of anatomy, like that of too many musical analysts, tends to be not merely obscure but chilling. Nevertheless a certain amount of jargon is inescapable for there are aspects of music which only a technical word can accurately describe. (For instance, one cannot describe a semitone as 'a narrow interval' and leave it at that.) Where such terms appear I shall always attempt to clarify them; I make no apology for this since I am directing my thoughts to the uninformed listener, who, realising that there must be more to music than meets the ear, wishes to have that elusive 'more' revealed.

Part One

1 _Beginners please _____

Since scientific observation has now shown that a child reacts to music even while in the womb, it is safe to assume that music elicits a fundamental response in humankind. There are many recorded instances of prodigiously gifted children who take to an instrument so naturally that it seems almost to be an extension of themselves. The problems ordinary mortals experience in acquiring the necessary skills of co-ordination to play even reasonably well seem not to exist for these prodigies. Even the genetic inheritance of such a gift is sometimes hard to trace, although it is more usual for a musical talent to be handed on directly from one generation to another. (Look up the name of Johann Sebastian Bach in a musical encyclopaedia and you will find that his family consisted of a virtually unbroken line of professional musicians for more than two hundred years.) But we do not need to travel back in time to seek examples of the passing on of talent from parent to child: the Oistrakhs, the Torteliers, the Kleibers, Shostakoviches or Ashkenazys of this world give ample contemporary evidence of the phenomenon. In other cases though, the gift seems just to appear, and mystified parents wonder how to cope with something almost beyond their comprehension.

Within these pages we do not need to concern ourselves with these unnaturally gifted creatures. For most of us, first musical experiences come in primary school where with much concentration (as well as great satisfaction) children learn to play tuned percussion instruments, recorders and even string instruments from an early age. These group activities are enormously beneficial, but there is one interesting deduction to be made from observing a number of such groups over the years. The quality of their performance seems to depend far more on the ability of the teacher to inspire enthusiasm than on any innate aptitude in the children. In other words, given a good teacher, you can produce remarkable results with children regardless of environment or family background. It seems to me to be relatively unimportant whether they perform in a steel band, on hand-bells, percussion instruments, consorts of recorders, jazz groups or even (as I have seen) on reconstructions of medieval instruments made by the children themselves. The great thing is to have the advantage of a communal musical experience at an early age, for it is in those formative years that the seeds of a genuine interest in music can best be planted.

During the last two decades or so there has been a positive explosion of musical activity in schools. Even the most academically conservative Heads are beginning to realise that music is more than a mere decoration on the school curriculum, to be encouraged in the children's spare time but not as a regular part of the syllabus.

Apart from any artistic or spiritual gain, communal music-making is one of the best forms of imparting discipline in the true sense, *self*-discipline, for each performer must play the right note at the right time at the right volume, a combination of demands which can be achieved only with real concentration. Watch the faces of children playing in such groups and you will seldom see attention wander. It is from such beginnings that the truly remarkable youth orchestras that have gained so much acclaim in recent years have grown, while the amazing standard of performance that is displayed in such national competitions as the BBC Young Musician of the Year could not possibly be achieved without a genuinely favourable climate for music-making of every kind. The opportunity to participate actively in music from an early age is in fact by far the best pathway to take towards a true comprehension of what music involves, its skills, its disciplines and its rewards.

Sadly there are generations of adults who never had such advantages; they may envy the young of today and in doing so they are tacitly admitting their own loss. However, when the famous Japanese violin teacher Suzuki insisted that the pupil's mother should not only attend the child's lessons but learn to play the instrument as well (thus sharing the early travail with far greater understanding and sympathy) he showed the high value he placed on parental involvement. Indeed I would say that one of the best ways for the uninitiated adult to cultivate a greater enjoyment of music is to take an active part in the rehearsals of a school orchestra. What in the early stages may seem little more than a glorified caretaker's job, pushing chairs about, putting up music stands and sorting out music, may, if he stays and listens, provide real insight. Any complex apparatus is easier to understand if one can first see it assembled from its component parts;

music is no exception. For this reason it is more instructive to attend the rehearsals of a youthful or amateur orchestra rather than a professional one.

To witness the London Symphony Orchestra rehearsing may be a privilege, but the standard of performance is such that to the layman even a first read-through would seem to leave little room for improvement. Most of the discussion between conductor and players would be incomprehensible, concerned as it would be with the finer points of technique. The string section of an orchestra is obsessed with the question of bowing, whether the stroke of the violin-bow should travel upwards or downwards, which *part* of the bow should be used to produce the required sound, whether the bow should remain in contact with the string or be allowed to bounce, and so on. While it is true that such questions must also be asked and answered in a youth orchestra, the reasons for the conductor's ruling will be made far clearer when the players are inexperienced since he will actually have to explain them; the initially bored parent, sitting overcoated in the half-empty hall surrounded by cast-off anoraks and battered instrument cases, will suddenly find that he is becoming absorbed as the first somewhat chaotic sounds begin to take recognisable shape.

I remember having a conversation some years ago with a garage foreman who I am sure had never been to a Beethoven sonata recital in his life. The previous evening on TV Barenboim had been holding a master-class for talented students. My mechanical friend had found it fascinating.

'There was this girl,' he said enthusiastically, 'Chinese I think she was, and she fairly ripped through that piece. And I thought to myself no one, but no one, could play it better'n that. And then this Barenboim fellow took over at the other piano and as soon as he started you could tell the difference. I don't know what it was, mind you, or how he did it, but you could tell all right. I suppose he just had Class and she didn't.'

One of the discoveries made through watching television is that rehearsals are often so much more intriguing than performances. To see Sir Geraint Evans taking students through a scene from an opera is not just to be let into the secrets of a master; it is a riveting experience even for those who would find the whole opera boring.

Seated in the opera theatre, possibly dragged there unwillingly by well-meaning friends, the musical tyro may well find the whole operatic experience too remote from reality. Why does it take so long for anything to happen?, he wonders; why must they sing all the time, and how can I be expected to follow when four of them are at it at once, all singing different words, and in *Italian* too . . . ? He can scarcely be blamed for preferring a good old-fashioned musical. Yet all his instinctive mistrust of the operatic art will be allayed by watching a student class profiting from Sir Geraint's expertise, or even, through the medium of television, to see a great producer working with singers of international calibre.

Here, then, is one significant and easily available step to take along the pathway to musical enlightenment – to take every opportunity to watch such programmes, absorbing as they are, but also to find time to sit in at the rehearsals of any tolerably good youth orchestra. Join me now in a visit to just such an occasion.

The scene is a large rectangular hall with a platform at one end; tall windows to the left give a view of a tarmac playground, around which are clustered several buildings of clearly different periods, showing that the school has been developed piecemeal rather than planned as a cohesive unit from the start.

Since the stage is not large enough to accommodate the orchestra, which appears to number some 70 players ranging in age from diminutive ten-year-olds to near-adults, the orchestral stands have been set out on the floor in an approximate fan-shape. The noise is considerable as chairs are pushed gratingly across the floor, brass players warm their instruments by blowing insecure fanfares, percussionists move their engines of destruction into place, children chatter, and, dominating the scene (though at this stage treated with little respect) the conductor, clapping his hands loudly in a rather vain attempt to gain control.

'Trumpets, move along a bit will you – no, not that way you clots! Over there, so as to make a bit more room for the timpani. What's that, Clare? You've left your part at home? Well go and ask Miss Stebbing if she's got one going spare.'

Getting everyone into place takes quite a few minutes (even with professional orchestras, dare I say!) but at last everyone seems to have settled. The air is filled with chaotic sound; it seems we are in a musical madhouse in which every player is pursuing an individual course, some in earnest, some merely releasing inhibitions by playing as loudly as they can. More handclaps from the conductor; a reluctant silence.

'O.K. Terence, give us an A, one of your better ones please.'

The oboe player looks at his instrument with an expression of distaste, sucks the reed a few times and at last commits himself to a long sustained note. At once the entire string section, violins, violas, cellos and double basses, begins tuning vigorously, soon to be joined by deafening blasts from brass and wind instruments.

'Not yet, brass,' yells the conductor; 'give the strings a chance.'

The strident sound of open strings tuned in bare fifths continues, as though a monstrous swarm of giant wasps had invaded the school precincts. At last the players are satisfied that their instruments are tolerably in tune and the sound dies away.

'Right, Terry, give us another one for the wind only –WIND ONLY I said, brass, so just shut up for a minute.'

After some thought, as though he had momentarily forgotten the proper fingering, Terence gives birth to another A, whereupon a bevy of flutes, oboes, clarinets, bassoons and even a shrill piccolo not only take the note from him but launch into a veritable cascade of scales, arpeggios and impromptu fantasies. (It is a fact of musical life that no orchestral player is ever content just to take the A proffered by the oboist; he seems to feel that he must see if the instrument is still actually in working order since he last played it a few moments previously.)

The avian bedlam dies as if on cue. This time the conductor simply gives Terence a nod; another A is forthcoming, unleashing a fusillade from the brass.

'Trumpets, can you come up a bit? You're still flat.'

'It's cold, Sir.'

'Well, stick 'em under your armpits or something, but let's try to play in tune.'

There is a clatter of footsteps and a girl hurries across the hall, nervously extricates her violin from its case and, to an accompaniment of derisive comments from her fellow-musicians, stumbles into her place in the fourth desk of the second violins.

'Late again, Janet,' says the conductor, arms folded, though his baton is already in his hand.

'Sorry Sir, it's the bus,' says Janet, flushing scarlet; and as discreetly as possible she takes an A from her neighbour.

'Right, perhaps now we're all here we could actually make a start. The work – and don't let anyone dare to tell me they haven't got a part – the work is Beethoven's Fifth Symphony. I expect you all think you know it, but you'll soon find you don't. I'll take it quite steady, but it'll still be one-in-a-bar; about this speed – ONE – ONE – ONE Ta-ta-ta-TAA – ONE Ta-ta-ta TAAAA – Got it?'

The orchestra nods assent; violins are tucked under chins, cello bows held at the ready; the brass players sit back, resigned to a period of silence before they are due to make an entry. At this point, since you may be beginning to wonder why I have brought you here at all, let us pause for a moment to take in all the implications of what we have seen so far.

The casual observer may feel that there is nothing especially remarkable about seeing a horde of children clambering into place and blowing or scraping a motley collection of instruments. But how was this collection arrived at, and why these particular instruments? Why are they sitting grouped as they are, violins to the conductor's left, cellos and basses to his right, violas (usually somewhat scarce) more or less in front of him? Is there any logic in the positioning of the wind, and if the trumpets and trombones are over there on the right, why are the horns so far away from them on the left?

We will return to the rehearsal later, but for the time being let us leave Mr Roberts, our conductor, baton poised to launch the orchestra into those awe-inspiring opening bars. The moving picture freezes in its frame; it is time for a brief excursion into musical history, and even a slight brush with acoustic science.

2 _Sources and resources _____

The orchestra as we know it today took a long time to evolve, even though the four 'families' – strings, wind, brass and percussion – have existed in one form or another for literally thousands of years. Musical instruments were made and cherished in the most ancient civilisations, while the scientific principles of acoustics had been discovered as early as the sixth century BC. No doubt the first discovery of variable pitch came to primitive man by accident, whether by tapping the sides of a gourd and finding that the sound changed in pitch as the level of the water altered, or by becoming aware that sticks of different lengths emitted different tones. Certainly the basic principle 'short means high, long means low' must have been understood before anything we would remotely acknowledge to be a musical instrument had been made. Even today, in a world dominated by the electronic marvels of computer and micro-chip, an infant child will take pleasure in hearing the pitch of the 'glug-glugs' rise as water is poured from one container to another. To the distraction of his parents, he will enjoy banging a drum, often with a surprisingly steady beat, or listen with delight to the rising pitch of steam coming from the spout as the kettle comes to the boil.

Is there a child who, given the chance, will not enjoy dragging a stick along a line of iron railings? Nor can children resist experimenting with resonance and echo effects if they are in tunnels or underpasses. To this extent then, we are fascinated with sound from infancy. Indeed, sound is so integral a part of our lives (except for the tragically afflicted deaf) that it is hard to realise that in one sense sound does not exist.

If, as the pessimists believe, we are going to end up by destroying ourselves in a nuclear holocaust, and if the destruction is so comprehensive that all human and animal life is terminated, then there is a good chance that the final delayed-action nuclear bomb will explode in complete silence.

This paradox is best explained by considering such everyday

objects as a radio or television set. Suppose that we stand in a room containing both. Turn to the radio; look at it hard and long; *will* it to give forth music. No matter how hard you concentrate, it will remain silent. Bring it to life by switching it on, and it will instantly oblige by giving us a wide choice from many and distant lands. Now we readily accept that a wireless transmitter sends out 'waves' that the human ear cannot pick up; but our radio set 'hears' those waves and transforms them into sound waves which we *can* hear. Similarly a television mast beams out a signal which our eyes cannot see; but our television set can 'see' the signal and translate it into light waves which our eyes can then interpret for us. It follows, therefore, that the process is three-fold; there must be an *initiator* which sets a wave in motion, a *carrier* (the radio wave, the television signal or the vibrations of the air which we call sound waves) and the *receiver*, whether it be a radio or television set or the human ear.

Neither the radio nor the television can 'hear' sound waves; their receivers are not designed to do so. The ear, be it animal or human, is equipped with a highly sensitive receiver (the 'drum') which not only picks up sound waves but passes them on to the brain for interpretation. It is the brain that tells us whether we are hearing speech, music, rain falling or the smash of broken crockery in the kitchen. If the sounds we hear are outside the brain's vocabulary, it cannot help us; hence our inability to understand a foreign language even though we hear it perfectly well.

To return, though, to that final cataclysmic explosion after all life has been destroyed. Undeniably it will be a violent *initiator*: it will set up huge vibrations in the air which will travel immense distances; but with no ears left to receive those vibrations and translate them, they will merely continue on their way until they pass beyond the fringe of our atmosphere, at which point, there being no air left, the vibrations will finally cease, still unheard and therefore technically 'silent'.

This brief excursion into the theoretical basis of sound may have seemed to have brought us a long way from the orchestra; but it is pointless to discuss instruments unless we have at least some notion of their common function. All instruments are designed with the same purpose in mind. Primarily they are initiators, setting a sound wave in motion so that anyone within range can receive and interpret the vibrations. They alter the pitch of the note by changing the *speed* of the vibrations; they alter the volume of the note by increasing or diminishing the *size* of the sound wave; they alter the quality of the note by changing the *shape* of the sound-wave. Here in diagrammatic form are the sound-waves created by four different instruments, each playing the same note.

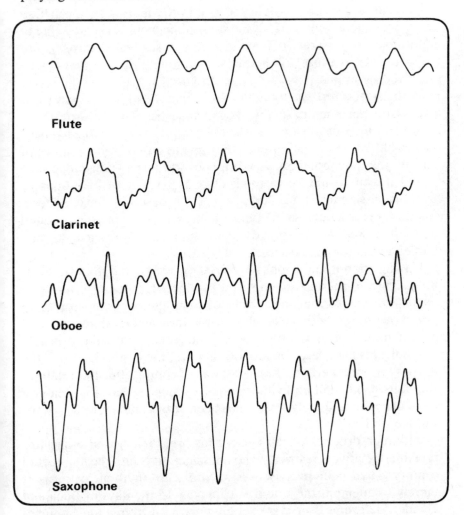

Fig. 1

The general outline with all the more decorative aspects removed can be seen to be the same, since each graph represents the same pitch; but it is the detailed variations, the decorative aspects, that translate into visual terms the different tone-colours that we associate with the four instruments. These variants are so subtle that if one were to take oscillographs of four different clarinettists each playing the same note, each would produce a different 'tone-print'. To put this into human terms, ask six people in a room to say in turn a single word such as 'dandelion' while you listen without looking. Even if, so far as is possible, they say it at the same pitch, you will still be able to identify each speaker. (There are now machines that recognise 'voice-prints' as a form of identification, though whether they can be deceived by mimicry has not been disclosed.)

Perhaps one further point should be made before we leave this necessarily perfunctory survey of basic acoustics. The patterns traced on an oscilloscope as shown in the diagram above are liable to give a somewhat false impression since they aim to give a visible reading of an invisible phenomenon. A more accurate way of imagining how sound travels would be to think of it as a series of pulsations or tremors passing along a coiled spring. (For those who have the taste for it, there are a number of books which explore the physics of sound in such a way as to spread satisfaction amongst scientists and bafflement among musicians.)

Having established, I hope not too laboriously, what sound *is*, let us now return to the instruments that produce it. It seems sensible to begin with percussion since drums of some kind are common to all primitive races, whether as hollowed-out logs, animal skins stretched over a frame, or as gourds. As with all instruments, the principle 'small means high, large means low' applies; the larger the drum, the deeper the note. Perhaps the easiest way of appreciating the relationship between sound and vibration is to watch the surface area of a large drum immediately after it has been struck; the vibration of the surface is clearly visible.

Although drums have an ancient history, their use in orchestras remained relatively restricted and unimaginative until the nineteenth century. Their main purpose was to emphasise rhythmic patterns or merely to augment the sound at climaxes. In the days of Bach and Handel the drums used were simply borrowed from a local detachment of cavalry and were virtually identical to those we can still see today played by the mounted drummer who leads the ceremonial processions of royalty from Buckingham Palace to the Abbey or the Houses of Parliament. Such drums could not be tuned except by varying the size of the metal bowl, from which the name **kettledrum** is derived. The normal eighteenth-century practice was to equip an orchestra with a pair, one to play the 'key' note of the scale, the so-called 'tonic', the other to play the fifth note, the 'dominant'. In due course it was discovered that the pitch of a drum could be varied by tightening or slackening the skin, since the true function of the bowl was to act as a resonator. A system of screws was devised, placed at regular intervals around the rim of the drum-head. Manipulated by hand, they enabled the player to change the pitch by several tones (degrees of the scale), although the slacker the head became, the greater the loss of quality. Such drums, or timpani to use the proper term, may still be seen today from time to time in amateur orchestras lacking the resources to equip themselves with the most recently developed instruments. These are technological marvels in which levers operated by a pedal (not unlike the clutch of a car) stretch or slacken the head to order. There is even a device attached to the side which, by measuring the tension, shows the timpanist which degree of the scale has been arrived at. However, despite these mechanical improvements, the orchestral timpanist will still probably require three, four or even five timpani to cope with the demands of some twentieth-century scores, since the best quality of sound in each instrument can be found only within a relatively small range.

Seated at the back of the orchestra surrounded by a set of gleaming copper instruments, the timpanist presents a commanding figure; but do not make the mistake of assuming that he has an undemanding job. Playing the timpani is a highly skilled art, requiring supple wrists, immaculate timing and the keenest of ears.

Alongside him in a position of vantage will be his colleagues in the percussion section playing a variety of instruments, most of which would have been unknown to a composer of Beethoven's era. His optimum demand was for timpani, bass drum, cymbals and triangle. The last three were reserved for special effects, sometimes referred to as 'Turkish' music, thereby acknowledging their exotic quality. Mozart, always keen to exploit any musical novelty, had employed them in his opera *Il Seraglio*; more remarkable, so enchanting is the effect, is his use of a little chime of bells in *The Magic Flute*. Such a sound was scarcely to reappear in music until Tchaikovsky, bewitched by the newly invented **celesta**, wrote the instantly recognisable 'Dance of the Sugar-Plum Fairy' in the *Nutcracker Suite*.

Nowadays no percussion section in a full symphony orchestra would be complete without a **glockenspiel** (lit. 'play of bells'), a set of tuned metallic bars of relatively high pitch and laid out in a manner comparable to a piano keyboard; a **vibraphone**, which might be described as a deeper-voiced glockenspiel whose tone quality can be enhanced by a mechanically induced vibrato; a **xylophone**, similar in range to the vibraphone but having wooden bars instead of metallic ones, and equipped with hollow resonating tubes to improve its tonal quality; a **tam-tam** or large Chinese gong which can be used to most impressive effect either with a single blow or a 'roll' (rapid beating which if built up to the full, can reach the threshold of pain); **triangles** of various sizes; a **side drum**, **tenor drum** and **bass drum**; **cymbals** of different sizes; a set of **tubular bells**; not to mention a variety of exotica from Latin American countries and even, if called for, whistles, revolvers, whips (two pieces of wood, hinged together, which can be 'clapped' to produce a sharp crack), anvils, chains or large wooden mallets. It is interesting to note that the percussion section, theoretically the most ancient and primitive, is the one area of the symphony orchestra in which the most spectacular change has been wrought in the twentieth century. The players must be masters of many skills, exceptionally alert, and even nimble of foot since it is often necessary to move from one instrument to the other, counting the silent bars as you go.

The second oldest family in the orchestra must be the woodwind, all instruments that despite their mechanical complexity are basically derived from the hollow reed stalk on which in far distant times some bored shepherd boy may have chanced to blow. Indeed, the oldest instuments known to man are tiny bone-flutes dating back to the Glacial period, but since they have no traceable derivations I have given the percussion pride of place. Nevertheless, flutes of a sort were known in China 3,000 years ago as well as in India, and since at such a time the distance between the two countries would have made any form of communication extremely difficult, it may be supposed that the 'invention' of such instruments occurred independently in different parts of the world.

All wind instruments (with the exception of the organ, which is a cross between wind and keyboard), have one thing in common; the sound is brought to life by the player's own breath. He may blow across an aperture in the pipe, as most children quickly discover with empty bottles; he may blow directly into the pipe, as one does with a recorder or tin whistle, or he can blow through a very narrow gap between two reeds (**oboe** and **bassoon**) or a comparable gap between a single reed and the mouthpiece of the instrument (**clarinets** and **saxophones**). The breath of the player sets in motion the air that is already within the hollow stem of the instrument; if the stem or tube is long, the note produced will be low; if short, the note will be high and shrill. How, then, is it possible to play a wide range of notes on an instrument whose length remains constant? With great ingenuity ways have been devised to direct the air-column through a number of diversions, thus varying the length of its journey and thereby altering the pitch. The simplest way of doing this, still to be found on the recorder or penny whistle, was to cut a series of holes in the pipe which could be stopped or opened by the player's finger-tips. But the limited span of the human hand automatically put a limitation on the length of such an instrument and therefore on its range. Hence the system of keys and rods that can be clearly seen nestling close to the main stem of instruments such as the clarinet or oboe. They may legitimately be regarded as extensions of the player's fingers, enabling him to keep his hands in a constant position as he holds the instrument to his lips.

The individual characteristics of the sound that distinguishes flute from oboe, or clarinet from bassoon, are governed by a number of factors such as the material of which the instrument is made, the shape of the bore or tunnel in which the air vibrates, and, harder to explain, the actual components of the sound known as the Harmonic Series. It has long been known that what we see as 'white' light can be shown by analysis to consist of violet, indigo, blue, green, yellow, orange and red; literally 'all the colours of the rainbow'. Now, in sound there is what we might refer to as a Tonal Spectrum. Absolutely pure sound, which can be produced in a laboratory, is dull and without appeal; it is roughly comparable to completely tasteless food.

Every note that we would classify as musical actually has a number of component parts, known suitably enough as 'partials'. It is the greater or lesser predominance of these that gives the note its 'flavour'. These partials taken in order form the harmonic series already mentioned. It is hard at first to accept that the C below the bass stave (two octaves below 'middle' C on the piano) actually has as one of its components a faint touch of the C four octaves higher, even though to our ears it is indisputably a 'low' note. Here, exposed to view, is the Tonal Spectrum of that same 'low' C.

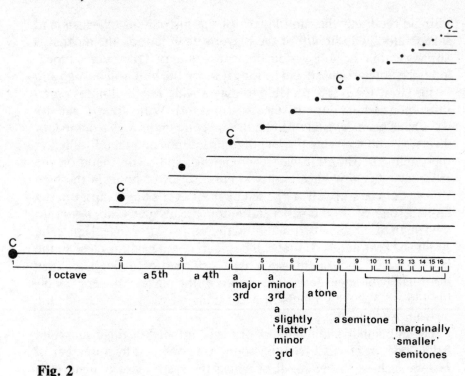

Fig. 2

Each line and each space on this grid represents a rising degree of the scale. It will be seen that the Cs correspond to the numerals 1, 2, 4, 8 and 16, an arithmetical progression of duplication.

The intermediate or 'upper' partials increase in number the further they get from the 'fundamental' note, the starting point. The distance between these remote upper partials decreases marginally at every remove until, beyond the 15th partial (No. 16) they become not only inaudible but virtually indistinguishable. It should be remembered that although for the sake of clarity the diagram shows a horizontal concept, in fact all the components sound simultaneously with the initial impact of the basic note.

I would not burden the reader with these rudiments of acoustic theory if they did not have a very vital relevance to actual musical experience. The expert eye of the physicist who has studied these matters can relate the sound-wave patterns shown on p. 11 to our graph of upper partials. By doing so he can deduce that the tone quality of a flute shows an absence of odd-numbered partials while only three even-numbered partials are present in any strength; the tone of the flute on 'middle' C is consequently bland and lacking in richness.

Our second example, the clarinet, shows a number of small kinks crowded closely together, evidence of a greater concentration on the high partials; it is this emphasis that gives the clarinet its somewhat 'reedy' tone. Not to labour the point, the oscillographs of the oboe and saxophone show different emphases, 'highlights' in the Tonal Spectrum which again impart the special timbre that we associate with each instument.[1]

In case this all seems to belong more to the laboratory than the concert-hall, let us turn our attention to the brass instruments, for it is in this section of the orchestra that the harmonic series reveals itself to be far more than a mere scientific analysis of the components of musical sounds. As with the percussion and wind families, the history of brass, or at any rate metal instruments, stretches far back in time.

The silver trumpets found in Tutenkhamun's tomb can still be played, though the sound may not be as thrilling as our imaginations would wish. (The 'trumpets' that supposedly caused the walls of Jericho to crumble were in all probability rams' horns.) But in all metallic instruments of the trumpet and horn variety there lurks a strange inner life. Insert a mouthpiece, for comfort's sake, into one end of a long metal tube, place your lips against its aperture and blow, not as you would to extinguish a candle, but rather as a small boy imitates the sound of a car engine or, less politely, 'blows a raspberry'. If you have sufficient skill to vary the ways in which your lips vibrate, you will discover that within the tube are to be found the first ten notes, or perhaps more, of the harmonic series. The different notes are conjured from the instrument entirely by adjustment of the player's mouth. According to the length of the tube, you will have an instrument that sounds a harmonic series 'in D' or 'in G' or whatever key you choose, given a hacksaw and willingness to experiment. Two problems arise. First, since it is easier to release all the notes from their metal prison if the tube is a long one, it is likely to be unwieldy, and hard to keep in proper contact with the lips; secondly the chosen harmonic series limits the player to one key only. A trumpet that is naturally tuned in D will be of little use in a Symphony in C.

[1] Acknowledgments to Alexander Wood, *The Physics of Music*.

The first problem was relatively easy to solve. We have all seen pictures of the old-fashioned post-horn or coaching-horn, usually on Christmas cards; or we may have seen the real article hanging decoratively on the wall of an old inn. It was soon discovered that it made no difference to the tonal quality of the instrument to curl it up into a more compact shape. The **trumpet** was re-shaped into a sort of oblong with curved ends, while the longer (and consequently deeper) **horn** was wound into a coil that the huntsman could conveniently sling on one shoulder.

The second problem, that of key, was initially solved in a fairly crude way. Either the player would have several instruments, or he would change the overall length of the tube by the insertion of a 'crook', a closely sleeved extension that lengthened, therefore lowering, the tube. Thus he could convert a trumpet 'in D' into a trumpet 'in C'.

It is worth mentioning that in the time of Bach and Handel the D trumpet was the one most generally available; consequently almost every chorus of rejoicing or triumph would automatically be written in D. The Sanctus in Bach's Mass in B minor or the 'Hallelujah' Chorus in Handel's *Messiah* demonstrate the point admirably.

It was in the early part of the nineteenth century that valves and pistons began to make crooks obsolete. There is no need to go into the mechanics of it here; suffice it to say that the use of valves enabled the player to divert the air-stream through a different route. Three valves on a horn (pistons on a trumpet) were enough to bring the full range of chromatic notes into play; at once horn and trumpet parts became more significant and more varied so that the way a composer like Tchaikovsky uses them is infinitely more enterprising than would have been practical for Beethoven.

Before we leave the subject of trumpets, there is one intriguing mystery that has never been adequately explained. Why are the trumpet parts in Bach's choral and orchestral works so much more challenging than those to be found in the music of Haydn or Mozart? The assumption most generally accepted is that there was a highly specialised Guild of Trumpeters who had mastered the technique of playing very high and remarkably rapid passages even without the aid of pistons. For some reason the secret was not passed on to a new generation; within a short time the special skill vanished, and for quite a long period afterwards trumpet and horn parts became the least interesting aspect of any orchestral score.

The **trombone**, direct descendant of the ancient sackbut, has a unique way of varying its harmonic series. The use of a slide enables the player to extend the length of the tube through seven positions, in each one of which a different harmonic series can be obtained. It has a big brother, the bass trombone; but nowadays, with recent improvements to the mechanism, the normal 'tenor' trombone has acquired a substantial number of extra notes in its lowest register, and the difference between tenor and bass is more one of quality than of compass.

The true bass to the orchestral brass is the **tuba**. It is a relative newcomer to the scene, dating only from the second half of the nineteenth century. The largest one, were it to be uncoiled, would be some sixteen feet (five metres) long, but they come in several sizes, the smaller ones usually being referred to as euphoniums. Like the trumpet it has piston-type valves, although in some instruments a rotary valve is preferred. It is a gentle giant capable of beautifully sonorous but surprisingly hushed tones if required. Its convincing representation of a foghorn in the closing scene of Britten's *Peter Grimes* is a classic instance of truly imaginative orchestration, infinitely more moving than a taped reproduction of an actual foghorn could ever be.

And so we come at last to the 'strings', the main body of the orchestra for over three centuries. Although it may seem irreverent to refer to a **violin** as a 'fiddle', the word is actually derived from the thirteenth-century *fidel*, a European adaptation of the Arabian *rebec*. However the basic idea of stretching gut-strings over a hollow resonating box had been thought of many centuries before, and I have seen something that looks remarkably like a square violin in an Egyptian wall-painting.

It should be made clear that the string itself is not responsible for the sound. Stretch a violin string between two nails hammered into a solid plank and, saw away at it as you will with a bow, you will obtain nothing but a rather unpleasant scraping sound that will soon put your teeth on edge. Attach that same string to a violin, set it vibrating by passing the bow to and fro across it, and those same vibrations will be transmitted through the 'bridge' (a small piece of fretted wood) to the 'belly'. The body of the violin simply acts as an amplifier, the vibrations being further transmitted from 'belly' to 'back' by means of a sound-post, a small wooden pillar, invisible from outside. The quality of the tone depends not only on the materials of which the instrument is made but also on the skill of the player who, by using a technique known as *vibrato* (a sort of trembling at the top of the finger in contact with the string) adds warmth and intensity to what would otherwise be a rather uninteresting sound. Listen to a violinist tuning his instrument; he will be playing the strings 'open', that is to say untouched by the fingers of his left hand. The resultant tone is quite different in quality from that produced by 'stopped' or fingered notes. The rather tinny nasal sound produced by youthful violinists in the early stages is due almost entirely to the absence of vibrato.

Apart from the way in which the sound is actually produced, there is another fundamental difference between the string family and the other instruments of the orchestra. Although both wind and brass instruments can play out of tune (flat if cold and sharp if too warm), the skilled player makes the more refined adjustments of pitch by his *embouchure*, the relationship of his lips and mouth to the instrument. The string player must create his own intonation. Suppose that he starts on the 'open' string A. By placing his first finger in firm contact with the string approximately an inch from its far end, he will in effect shorten the string, thereby raising its pitch to B. If he then presses the next finger on to the string at a distance of roughly half an inch, he will produce the note a semitone (or *half*-tone) higher, C. But if he places the finger approximately an inch away, he will produce a note a *tone* higher, C sharp as it is called. (C♯). As he progresses further along the string the distances required to distinguish between tones and semitones continually diminish by very fine degrees until, at the highest part of the string, the fingers must be bunched really closely together.

To demonstrate just how accurate the player's judgement must be, it is worth considering the problem of octaves, the paired notes C–C, D–D and so on, eight notes apart. If a pianist plays a descending scale in octaves with one hand, his thumb and fifth finger will remain an absolutely constant distance apart. Now a skilled violinist can also play octaves by stopping the lower note on one string with his first finger and the upper note on the adjacent higher string with his fourth finger. It's an awkward stretch, but it can be done. Suppose now that he is required to descend step by step through four consecutive octaves. The distance between his first and fourth finger must change fractionally for each octave in turn, widening almost imperceptibly to the eye. Correspondingly, if he plays an ascending passage in octaves, the distance between the fingers must narrow. Such fine adjustments demand endless, patient practice, the problem of intonation being common to all string instruments.

If the violins are the 'sopranos' of the string section, the **violas** are the 'altos' – indeed the instrument is actually called 'alto' in French. Slightly larger bodied than the violin, it is tuned a fifth lower; in other words, its three higher strings, G, D, A correspond exactly to the three lower strings of the violin. Because of its larger body, with consequently a greater hollow space inside, the tone quality is darker, more mellow.

There is a rather different overlap between viola and **cello** although the two instruments often play in the same range. The two upper strings of the cello are tuned a tone higher than the two lower strings of the viola. The strings of violin, viola and cello alike are tuned a fifth apart as the following chart shows:

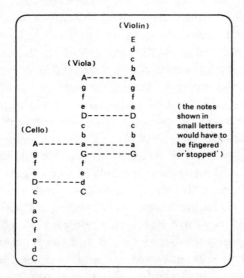

Fig. 3

The **double-bass**, deepest of the orchestral string family, is tuned in fourths since the great length of the string requires wider stretches between the fingers of the player. Bass players seldom use two adjacent fingers for consecutive notes except in the highest register. However one cannot be absolutely didactic about its tuning since some instruments have five rather than four strings. The most normal

arrangement is G
         D
         A
         E   with the option of going down to a low C by means of an extension. The 'high' G shown corresponds in pitch to the second lowest string on the cello, and it is unquestionably this over-lapping from one instrument to another as well as the shared method of tone-production that makes the string section the most homogeneous in blend.

The symphony orchestra that we see in a concert hall today or, for that matter, the youth orchestra to whose rehearsal I still intend to return, is very different in size and scope from anything Mozart or Haydn would have known. Although the concept of a number of musicians playing together is age-old, it was only through royal or aristocratic patronage that such groups could be kept together on any continuing basis. During the seventeenth century the maintenance of a 'house' orchestra became a notable status symbol, something akin, though considerably less costly, to keeping a string of racehorses today. Proficiency in music was considered a desirable attribute among the aristocracy and a composer such as Haydn would have been expected not only to write music to entertain his princely patron and his guests but to write pieces suitable for him to perform as well. Of all composers Haydn was perhaps the most fortunate in his employment, and for most of his adult life he was able to count on the resources of a resident orchestra attached to the sumptuous court of the Esterhazy family. However, to our eyes (and ears!) his orchestra would have seemed something of an economy pack with only six 'first' violins, four 'seconds', two violas, two cellos and two basses. Against this relatively puny number the wind and brass (usually borrowed from the military) must have seemed unduly powerful, especially in the resonant conditions to be found in a large but sparsely furnished salon. In the later years of his life, when he began to travel, Haydn must have been thrilled by the substantially larger orchestra that had been formed by a syndicate of wealthy music-lovers, *Le Concert de la Loge Olympique* which boasted forty violins and ten double-basses. It was for them that he wrote the so-called 'Paris' symphonies of 1785–6. Some five years later he made his first visit to London where he enjoyed the greatest popular success he had ever known; even so, the orchestra was not enormous, sixteen violins, four violas, three cellos, four double-basses, two each of the woodwind family, a pair of horns, two trumpets and a timpanist. Haydn directed the orchestra from a centrally placed piano, filling in the harmonies when he felt like it and doubtless correcting anyone who went astray by thumping out the right notes (see Fig. 4.)

All this was mere history until comparatively recent times when a keen interest in 'authentic' performance has increasingly been developed. It is now possible to hear eighteenth-century music much as it must have been played at the time; the problem for the listener is to equip himself with eighteenth-century ears, for it is hard to cleanse the mind of the sounds of the modern orchestra to which we have become so accustomed.

During the nineteenth century an increasingly prosperous middle class felt the need for the cultural entertainments that had previously been reserved for the aristocracy. What we might term 'public' orchestras came into being in most large cities. A mixture of amateur and professional players, their composition was consistent neither in numbers nor instrumental resources, but gradually a desirable norm was established. This would consist of between twenty and thirty violins, divided for musical reasons into 'firsts' and 'seconds', anything from six to ten violas, half a dozen cellos and four or five double-basses. The wind instruments would normally be in pairs, often with the less proficient player playing a subsidiary part, although oboes and bassoons were often present in what to us might seem surprisingly large numbers – as many as five. Two (sometimes four) horns and two trumpets would make their considerable – if musically rather uninteresting – contribution, reinforced by a timpanist with two timpani.

The seating of the orchestra was the subject of much experiment, partly dictated by considerations of environment; opera-pits or churches present obvious problems, while properly designed concert platforms with tiered seating were a relatively late development.[1] It was Haydn during his visit to London who established the general pattern that was increasingly accepted in the subsequent period. He arranged his players in a fan-shape (Fig. 4).

---

[1] To strike a personal and contemporary note, I can remember conducting the London Philharmonic Orchestra in a comprehensive school in London in the concert-suite from Bernstein's *West Side Story*. The cellos were seated at floor-level some five feet below me to my right, while the extensive percussion required were similarly placed to my left. I gave several vital leads with my left or right foot!

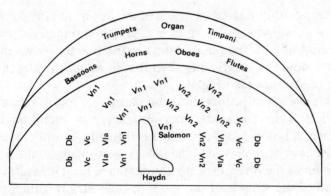

Fig. 4

The idea of placing the first and second violins so that they faced each other remained normal practice right into the twentieth century and is still preferred by some conductors, especially in works where there are musical exchanges between their respective parts; but the second violins are at a disadvantage since their instruments are projecting the sound *away* from the audience. It is almost entirely because of this that most orchestras today seat all the violins to the conductor's left.

The most curious and questionable aspect of Haydn's arrangement is the wide separation of the lower strings. Can the two double-basses at the extreme left have managed to synchronise their playing with their colleagues on the far side? It must have been very difficult, especially with the limited rehearsal time that seems to have been available. Although Haydn may have considered such a seating plan practical, clearly others didn't, and it was soon realised that better results could be obtained by keeping like with like.

Less than half a century later, the twenty-five-year-old Mendelssohn was appointed conductor of the Leipzig Gewandhaus Orchestra, reputed to be the first fully professional orchestra in history. Although the orchestra had been in existence for some time, it is interesting to note that he was the first of its conductors to use a baton. He arranged his orchestra as shown in Fig. 5.

This seems more logical than Haydn's approach, but it was still by no means standard. In 1846 the seating plan of the Philharmonic Society of London (which seemed to have suffered from a plethora of double-basses) was markedly different (Fig. 6). Notice how the tradition established by Haydn still lingered on in the separation of cellos and double-basses.

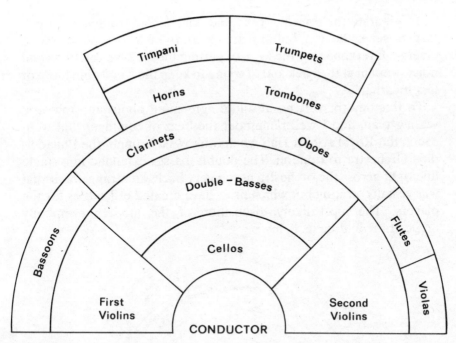

Fig. 5

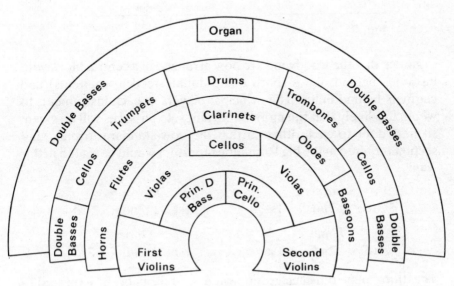

Fig. 6

To separate the principal cello and double bass from all their colleagues seems lunatic, but at least a pattern of sorts is beginning to emerge. Everyone sees the logic of putting the loud-voiced brass and noisy timpani at the back and of trying to keep the woodwind more or less together.

To this day there is no absolute agreement about an orchestral seating-plan, and I well remember the buzz of comment that went round the Royal Albert Hall when Stokowski brought the Philadelphia Orchestra to London. The double-basses extended in a single line right across the orchestra at the very back, an arrangement that was visually striking but which must have created difficulties for the players. The most likely disposition of the modern symphony orchestra would be as below:

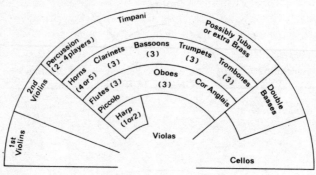

Fig. 7

Notice that the woodwind are now arranged in a central block with bassoons behind oboes (both being double-reed instruments) and clarinets behind flutes. The principal players of each instrument, to whom it is likely that the more important solo passages will be given, sit next door to each other so that the now standard 'triple' wind section required in the big Romantic repertory would be seated in this way:

	Clarinets			*Bassoons*	
3rd	2nd	1st	1st	2nd	3rd
	Flutes			*Oboes*	
3rd	2nd	1st	1st	2nd	3rd

The 'third' player in each group would most probably be expected to double on piccolo, cor anglais, bass clarinet and contra-bassoon although extra players may be engaged for works requiring large resources.

One may well be tempted to ask why the horns should be on the opposite side from their fellow brass players; indeed it is diplomatic for conductors never to refer to the horn section as brass. The reason is that their function often as not is to blend with the woodwind, which they prefer to do without feeling that there are trombones breathing down their necks.

Before we finally leave this game of Musical Chairs it is worth mentioning that in recent years composers have been increasingly intrigued by the refreshing possibilities of re-grouping the instruments entirely, perhaps forming them into small mixed groups to create new and unfamiliar blends of sonority. *Virages*, a remarkable work for solo cello and orchestra by Douglas Young, composed for the Leicestershire Schools Symphony Orchestra, divides the players into so many small groups that they are identified in the score by postal addresses such as N.W.3 or S.E.10, thus giving the conductor some assistance in at least knowing where to look!

3 _Sounds in the head _____

With an emphatic grunt Mr Roberts gives a sweeping downbeat with his baton and the hall is suddenly filled with the explosive sound of Beethoven's mighty opening phrase.

'Hold it till I bring you off!' he shouts as the players come to the second sustained note. 'Now quiet strings, and no crescendo till it says so.'

For the next twelve bars the strings *ta-ta-ta-taa* along their way with tolerable accuracy, until with a somewhat wild wave of his arm the conductor endeavours to bring in as one man flutes, oboes, clarinets, horns, trumpets and timpani. The three karate-like chords that cut off the phrase are distinctly ragged.

'Not together!' comes the angry reprimand. 'Those chords must be really short, aggressive, as though Beethoven was giving you a punch on the nose.'

A few children dutifully titter at this example of scarcely Beecham-esque wit. Mr Roberts, no Sir Thomas as he would willingly admit, turns to the violins.

'Firsts, you are the only ones to hold on to that top G there in the pause bar. Sally, show them how to do it . . .'

The leader, clearly a gifted girl who passed her Grade VIII with Distinction and has put in for a place at the Royal College, turns towards the pack behind her and plays the four-note chord confidently, sustaining the top note with a full bow and plenty of vibrato.

'Good girl,' says Mr Roberts approvingly. 'Now everyone, let's just have those last three bars before the pause-bar, ta-ta-ta TUM-TUM-TAAA. And wind, you've got to be really on the ball there or you'll always sound late. Come in smack after the beat. Right, three bars before the pause-bar; got it? Watch!' Another emphatic downbeat and Beethoven is brought somewhat shakily to life once more. 'Trumpets, you're LATE! A-GAIN everybody.' This time it fares better and they push on into the thunderous unison that follows the pause.

To build up a performance of such a work from scratch (well chosen word!) is an arduous and painstaking business, demanding unflagging enthusiasm from the conductor and conscientious patience from the players. Their reward is in the doing of it, the gradual falling into place of all the details, the sense of growing achievement and the possibly almost unconscious awareness that they are performing something which represents a prodigious feat of human imagination. Perhaps as they plough their way uncertainly through the first movement we might give some thought to the act of composition. What is a composer, what does being a composer involve?

Composers are born not made; true, one can study composition, but unless the inborn talent is there, lessons are of little value except as a means of acquiring academic qualifications of doubtful worth. If the gift is there, it will probably reveal itself quite early in life and the child will be drawn to music by some inner compulsion that he or she may find hard to explain. One could perhaps describe the phenomenon as 'having sounds in the head', sounds which demand to be made manifest in some more tangible form. Before the necessary skill has been learnt to commit them to paper, it is probable that the child will resort to improvisation, discovering through practical experiment how to convert nebulous thought into actuality. It is in this early stage that an imaginative teacher can be of the greatest service, showing the sheer technicalities of musical notation as required, without at the same time circumscribing any natural invention by insisting on the observance of rules that have no real application to genuine creativity.

There are many instances of truly remarkable works written by composers in adolescence; Mozart, Schubert and Mendelssohn are the most generally acknowledged, with somewhat lesser figures such as Rossini, Bizet and even Korngold nudging them closely. Recently some quite extraordinary settings of *Four French Songs* by Benjamin Britten have come to light, written when he was only fourteen, but sounding like the work of a completely assured mature composer. Such prodigious gifts are rare, one need hardly say, although they usually indicate a natural facility in handling musical material that others of equal or even greater worth may not share. For instance, few would deny that Beethoven was a greater composer than Mendelssohn even though he found composition an infinitely more laborious process.

Now while we can watch fascinated as an artist works on a canvas or as a sculptor chisels away at a piece of wood, it is less rewarding to watch a composer at work or even, should he prefer to work at the keyboard, to listen to the birth-pangs of his latest creation. Asked on one occasion to define the act of composition, I described it as 'the identification of sounds half-heard'. It is a simplification of course, since one identified, the sounds must then be organised; their proper place must be found within the framework of the planned composition, their proper tone-colour allocated. One thing should be clarified before we attempt to explore this truly mysterious process; personal emotion has little to do with composition during the actual period of creativity. While it is true that the inner self may be given a jolt by some specific event, the death of a parent, a broken love affair, the feel of a landscape, the joy of spring, or even an imagined image such as 'the afternoon of a faun', once the notes begin to be committed to paper, a different process begins. The contrasts within any major work, whether symphony, concerto, quartet or sonata, are so extreme and rapid that to assume the composer experienced a comparable emotional change within himself at the moment of writing would make him a candidate for the madhouse.

One does not have to feel sad to write a sad tune, nor happy to write a joyful one; the means of expressing sadness or joy are part of music's vocabulary, upon which the composer can draw at will. Earlier in my life I wrote a great deal of incidental music for radio drama, plays and films, and it was my experience that as soon as I read the first pages of a script or saw the first rough cut of a film, sounds would come flooding into my mind as a spontaneous reaction. The image, written or visual, was the stimulus; however, to compose a work in the abstract, a sonata for instance, was a totally different experience, demanding a much longer period of gestation of which the conscious self was hardly aware.

I am convinced that most forms of artistic creativity take place beneath the layer of consciousness; once the pressure has built up sufficiently to force itself on the composer's attention, he will then feel the compulsive urge to direct the sounds on to the page. It seems that composers might well be divided into two categories, *compulsive* or *deliberative*. The compulsive composer, of which type Mozart and Schubert were supreme examples, is driven by an inner force which demands to be released regardless of environment, health, reward or even practicality. (Schubert continued to write symphonies despite the fact that they were never performed in his lifetime; Schoenberg took eleven years to compose the *Gurrelieder* which, from the start, he conceived on so vast a scale that he must have realised that the chances of actual performance would be negligible.)

The deliberate composer is one who, while aware of that same inner force, is able to direct it more consciously, even to summon it to order. Each of the several changes of idiom and purpose that one can perceive in various periods of Stravinsky's life was the result of a conscious desire to experiment. He once said that he preferred to think of himself as an 'inventor', a somewhat less emotive word than composer. Bach, when writing such amazing demonstrations of the composer's craft as the *Musical Offering* or *The Art of Fugue* was most certainly deliberative; but to write a work on the scale of the St Matthew Passion for the relatively sparse and amateurish resources at his disposal was compulsive, a testimony of his own devout faith with which he was more concerned to catch the ear of God than of an audience.

The inner force of which I have spoken might well be compared to a spring whose flow may vary from a flood to a trickle. For someone as neurotic and self-destructive as Tchaikovsky, composition was often a torment. In May 1888 he began work on what is probably the most popular of his symphonies, the Fifth; it was nearly ten years since he had successfully completed the Fourth, and although throughout that decade he had continued to compose prolifically, the symphony as a form still presented a daunting prospect. 'I am now slowly and laboriously beginning to squeeze a symphony out of my dulled wits' he wrote to his brother in May. Nearly a month later he was writing to Nadezhda von Meck, the patroness with whom he kept up a correspondence for years without ever wishing to meet her:

> I'm now going to work intensively as I'm terribly anxious to prove not only to others but also to myself that I'm not yet played out. I often have doubts about myself – hasn't the time come now to stop, haven't I always overstrained the imagination too much, hasn't the source dried up? For this must happen some time if I am destined to live another ten years or so, and how is one to know whether the time hasn't already come to lay down one's arms? I don't know if I told you that I've decided to write a symphony? At first it went rather slowly but now the inspiration seems to be forthcoming; we shall see. (*Eulenberg Miniature Score No. 429, trans. David Lloyd-Jones*.)

Some twelve days later he had actually finished the sketch of the whole symphony, although as yet it was still not orchestrated.

> It is difficult to say at the moment how my symphony has turned out . . . It doesn't seem to have the old lightness and constant flow of material. As I remember it, I used not to be so exhausted at the end of a day; now I am so tired each night that I am not even able to read.

And to think that the most physically wearing part of a composer's life, the arduous labour of making a fair and legible full score showing every instrumental part, still lay ahead.

Compare this now with Dvořák some four years later working on his 'New World' Symphony. He first put pen to paper on 10th January 1892. By the 21st he had sketched the whole of the first movement; four days later he had completed the second; by the end of the month he had raced on to the end of the third. Before embarking on the Finale he gave his creative self a rest (of sorts!) by scoring what he had already written. To give some indication of the extra labour involved and the inevitable slowing of pace once the sheer excitement of creation is over, this task took him from 9th February until 10th April. With other things on his mind, such as being Director of the National Conservatory of Music in New York, he delayed work on the Finale for a short period, but the sketch was completed by 12th May and the full score a mere twelve days later on 24th May.

I should perhaps elaborate for a moment on the word 'sketch'. The most famous sketches are contained in a number of manuscript notebooks left by Beethoven. Invaluable source material for the scholar, they are for the most part almost valueless to anyone not intimately familiar with his works. Mostly fragments a few bars long, they often consist of ideas so banal that one is tempted to wonder why he bothered to write them down in the first place. It is rather as though a Shakespeare enthusiast were to discover a sheet of paper, authentically in the playwright's hand, reading like this:

> *To be?   Or not?   Question: is it ~~better~~ nobler to endure*
> *blows?   buffeting?   of ~~bad~~ ill luck or to fight back*
>   *fortune?*
> *against   slings and   arrows*
>   *end them how?   Death?   sleep?*
> *Dreams – bad dreams.   What happens when we die?   Stop and think.*

Who could possibly imagine that out of such chaos could emerge one of the greatest soliloquies ever written? Yet many of Beethoven's sketches bear no more resemblance to the final version than does this jumble of words to Hamlet's immortal meditation.

In this he was exceptional; while it may be true that many composers have captured the first intimations of a work in fragmentary form, I do not know of any other who was prepared to start from such unpromising materials. What Tchaikovsky and Dvořák meant by sketches may also be referred to as a 'short score.' All the main material of the movement is there, crammed on to two or three staves, as the five-line grids used in music are called. There will almost certainly be indications of the intended orchestration, here a line marked 'Horn solo', there a passage shown as 'full orch.' or 'str. only'. In extending this preliminary and time-saving sketch into a full score, the composer will have to use manuscript paper sufficiently large to allow room for the individual part allocated to each instrument in the orchestra from flute to double bass.

> Flutes
> Oboes
> Clarinets
> Bassoons
>
> Horns
> Trumpets
> Trombones (tenor)
>   (bass)
>
> Tuba
>
> Timpani
> Percussion
>
> Harp or harps
>
> Solo instrument or choral parts as needed
>
> Strings

Fig. 8

As is the case in every aspect of music, a long evolutionary process has been at work. For instance there was a time when it seemed logical to group all the 'high' instruments, flutes, oboes and violins, together at the top of the page, and to put the 'low' instruments, violas, cellos, bassoons and double basses at the bottom. In the latter part of the nineteenth century it gradually became the universal practice to group the instruments in families so that the conductor can more easily see at a glance in which area of the orchestra the main interest lies. The printed scores of works from earlier periods have been adjusted to fall in line with the general custom so that nowadays if one buys a minia-ture score of a Mozart piano concerto, one does not find the violin and viola parts at the top of the page, the wind in the middle, and the cellos, basses and timpani below the solo piano part. The accepted layout of an orchestral score is as shown in Fig. 8; but as I have indicated on p. 27, there has been a notable tendency to break up this conventional grouping in recent years, and the scores of *avant-garde* composers will invariably present a very different appearance, not only with regard to the layout of the orchestra but even the actual notation of the music.

With this in mind let us return now to the opening bars of Beethoven's Fifth Symphony. Rightly we think of them as awe-inspiring, a rugged statement of overpowering force, the more impressive for its stark simplicity. 'Thus Fate knocks at the door . . .', Beethoven is supposed to have said many years after the work was written; but since much nearer the time he had told the pianist Czerny that the little pattern of notes had come to him from a yellow-hammer's song, it is unwise to place too much faith in two attributions so diametrically opposed. It is more important to listen to the music than to ask what it is about. As was so often the case, Beethoven arrived at this seemingly simple concept by a roundabout route that included some almost unbeliev-able trivialities.[1] Let us draw a veil over them as Beethoven would have wished and accept the final version. I wonder how many people who have heard this, the best-known of all symphonies, on a number of occasions could honestly say that they know precisely which instru-ments play those opening bars. In fact, although many of us would be prepared to swear that at least some brass were involved, Beethoven uses nothing but strings and two clarinets. It is only after the pause-bar which young Sally demonstrated at our school rehearsal that the full orchestra blares out a more forceful version; had Beethoven used all his resources in the very opening bars, such greater emphasis would not have been available to him. Before we can explore this great work any further, the time has come to discover just what a symphony is.

[1] See Antony Hopkins, *The Nine Symphonies of Beethoven* (Heinemann, 1981).

4 __What's the form?

'Great! Great!' cries Mr Roberts enthusiastically as he flicks a few drops of sweat from his brow. 'At least, let's say it was distinctly recognisable. . . . Now remember, we'll do the repeat at the performance – and I trust you've all told your Mums and Dads to come on the day, October the eighteenth as you all know, so we haven't got all that long – but for the moment let's push on past the double bar into the Development. For goodness' sake, though, horns and clarinets mark REPEAT in your copies because if you come charging in when the strings have all gone back to the beginning, the whole thing will dis-in-te-grate!! O.K. – here we go, and horns, you can really belt this one out *fortissi-* MO!'

And so they do, instantly followed by a ferocious unison from the strings.

At this point our uninitiated listener, who has found himself becoming increasingly absorbed, begins to wonder what on earth Mr Roberts is talking about. Why should the players go back to the beginning and start again unless it is to give them a second chance if things have gone wrong? What is a 'double-bar'? What is the Development? And why does the conductor say '*fortissimo*' when all he seems to mean is 'very loud'?

This last question at least is simple to answer since Italian has been more or less accepted as a universal language for the indication of such matters as tempo, volume and the like. I say 'more or less' since there are always a few fervent nationalists who insist on giving such instructions in their own tongue, to the puzzlement of musicians from other nations. However, the other questions raised need far more thought.

Let us consider for a moment the essential difference between looking at a painting and listening to a piece of music. When we stand in front of a picture in an art gallery we can take in a general impression of its subject at a single glance, a landscape, a still life, a portrait, a scene from mythology. Then, if it has aroused our interest sufficiently, we can take as much time as we like to assimilate the details, the skill with which the artist has caught a reflection in the water, the way the figure on the left is balanced by the tree in the background to the right, the detail of the flowers at the water's edge which on close inspection seem to be mere blobs of paint but which from any distance seem to be clearly identifiable as irises, buttercups or cowslips. The point is that Time is under our control; we can stay and examine the picture for as long as we wish.

Imagine now that instead of a painting we are looking at a single frame from a cine film whose total duration is forty-five minutes. The image in itself may be as beautiful and as satisfying as a painting, but within the context of the film it is only a fleeting moment lasting a twenty-fourth of a second. By isolating a single frame we appear to be able to control Time, freezing the image; but once the film begins to pass through the projector, Time controls us and we must attend the order of events in their proper sequence. It is perfectly feasible to carry this analogy into music. I can still remember the sensation of almost incredulous delight I felt when, as a boy of sixteen, I started to read through a piano piece by Debussy called *Reflets dans l'eau*; while still groping my way uncertainly through the first page, I came across a sequence of four chords which were unquestionably the most sensuously beautiful that I had ever encountered. I was spell-bound by them, playing them time after time, savouring them as one might some delicious sweetmeat. My playing of one chord was directly comparable to looking at the single frame from a film; but in the context of the piece, that chord was a swiftly passing moment in a continuous flow of sound. Now, while we can see at a glance the whole content or shall I say 'plot' of a painting, we could not possibly work out the plot of a film by looking at a single frame; and while I could enjoy the sensation of a single chord in an impressionistic piano piece by Debussy, I could not deduce from that what might happen on page three or five or seven. During a performance we are not in control of Time; the music continues at its own pace as interpreted by the performer and we cannot cry 'Stop! Play that bit again . . .' (Incidentally that is precisely why I urge the musical novice to attend rehearsals because it *will* give him several opportunities to hear passages played again; moreover they will most probably be the very passages which, because of their inherent complexity, are likely to cause him some bafflement.)

As if composers were consciously aware of the problem imposed by our inability to arrest Time in its flight, a convention was established whereby in effect we *are* able to cry 'Play that again'. The repetition of even quite substantial sections of music came to be expected so that the listener might absorb the content, tucking away any outstanding features in the back of his mind for future reference. The point from which such a repetition was to be made is indicated by a double vertical line on the score, hence the term 'double bar'.

Time that is without any event to mark its passing can literally drive us mad, as experiments in sensory deprivation have shown. We have a deep-seated need to measure time, by minutes and hours, days and nights, by seasons, by birthdays or by generations. Form in music is a way of measuring Time; it gives us landmarks, points of recognition; it tells us when we can relax or when we are about to embark on a new venture; it gives us a feeling for proportion – is the scale of the music large or small? – and draws our attention to aspects of musical structure of which we might otherwise remain unaware.

The conventional text-book approach to the subject of Musical Form tends to suggest that it is far more rigid than the evidence would warrant. Even the single word Sonata covers an extraordinarily wide range of music, from compositions for brass ensemble by the early Italian composer Giovanni Gabrieli (?1557–1612) to a version for string orchestra of his own string quartet made by the late Sir William Walton. Between these rather uncharacteristic extremes are to be found literally thousands of works similarly called Sonata – sonatas for virtually every orchestral instrument (usually accompanied by piano), sonatas for harpsichord, for piano, for organ, for small groups of instruments, and even (by the Welsh composer Daniel Jones) a sonata for timpani. There are sonatas in one, two, three, four or five movements; there are sonatas that last less than five minutes or the best part of an hour. This extraordinary flexibility is easily explained since the literal meaning of the word is a 'sounding' piece, that is to say an instrumental work as opposed to a *cantata* which is a 'sung' piece, or vocal work. Where confusion is likely to arise is in grasping the difference between a sonata – a type of work – and sonata-form – a type of musical structure. For the most part all those sonatas most commonly performed, whether by Haydn, Mozart, Beethoven or Schubert, will probably have only one movement in sonata form, the first.

It may seem perverse of me, having focussed attention so strongly on the first movement of a symphony, now to appear to change tack and concentrate on sonatas; in fact this is not as illogical as it seems since symphonies are in effect sonatas for orchestra, while concertos are simply a further elaboration incorporating a soloist or soloists. Consequently it really is essential if we are to enjoy or comprehend such large-scale compositions, to have some conception of sonata form. It is true that we may often enjoy music purely for the sound it makes; but there is a lot more to music than mere sound. If sound were to be the only consideration, then music would be truly primitive, exploiting the simple and self-evident principles that loud quick noises are exciting, quiet slow ones soothing. Let us forget Beethoven for the moment and establish a few general principles.

Reduced to its bare essentials, a sonata-form movement will consist of three main sections; first, the Presentation of the material to be used, in which some fairly positive contrasts of mood need to be established; second the Development or extension of this material, into which quite new elements may well be introduced; third, a Re-assessment of the original material in the light of the experience gained during the central section. This third part is normally referred to as the Recapitulation, a somewhat misleading word in my view since it implies a too slavish repetition of what has gone before.

Let us now move from the language of music to the language of words and see if it is possible to construct a short story in sonata form:

[1] Roger Winyard opened the front door and went out into the street. [2] One could tell at a glance from his brisk walk and almost military bearing that he was a man of action who would brook no argument. [3] Even so, as he strode through the park to the block of flats where Stella lived he was not insensitive to the beauty of the banks of flowers whose brilliant summer hues made so bright a contrast to the drab grey of the tarmac path. [4] Once arrived at the southern fringe of the park, it was only a matter of moments before he reached Stella's apartment. [5] Hardly had he touched the bell when she opened the door.
'Roger darling', she said softly and then, reaching a slender arm around his neck, she clasped him fondly to her, murmuring endearments into his ear.
[6] Surprisingly he didn't respond as she expected him to; there was a cold aloofness about him that caused her to break away from him.
[7] With a slight frown she queried 'What is it, love – is something wrong?'
[8] 'I'll say there is', he replied, [9] firmly closing the door behind him.

Here is the Presentation of the material, or, to use the more commonly accepted term, the Exposition. Let us translate it into music, not actual notes but musical functions; we will assume it to be a piano sonata.

Sentence 1.
Establishes (Roger's) 'home', the so-called key of the sonata. (A major, C minor etc.) Going out into the street suggests a few introductory bars, not thematically important.

Sentence 2.
One can almost hear the music, brisk but not quite four-square enough to be an actual march. This is the First Subject, usually positive in character, Roger's theme.

Sentence 3.
Shows a modification of the above, introducing a more lyrical note; themes can easily be made to change their character by subtle modifications to harmony and rhythm.
The banks of flowers rising above the drab grey path would, in musical terms, consist of decorative and brilliant passages in the right hand over a conventional formula of repeated and relatively uninteresting chords in the left.

Sentence 4.
The 'arrival at the southern fringe' signifies that we are now in a new key; the journey through the park would be called a Bridge Passage and takes us from Roger's 'home' key, known academically as the Tonic, to Stella's 'home' key, known as the Dominant. The final and positive establishment of this new key, or Tonality, is liable to be swiftly accomplished, 'a matter of moments'.

Sentence 5.
'Hardly had he touched the bell', i.e. as soon as this new key has been stabilised: Stella's appearance establishes a different mood entirely, more alluring than Roger's almost military bearing. She represents the Second Subject, always a contrast to the first.

Sentence 6.
Roger's aloof reaction: elements of the First Subject reappear, creating a sense of resistance to the softened mood of the Stella theme.

Sentence 7.   'With a slight frown...' The Second Subject is
               tinged momentarily with a touch of a minor key; the
               phrases become questioning, brief, divided one from
               the other by silences, which, in music, always raise
               the question 'what is going to happen next?'

Sentence 8.   A sudden and fierce reiteration of the First Subject
               with, at 9, the closing of the door; in musical terms
               this is a firm 'cadence', establishing positively that we
               are now 'in' Stella's home key.

While it would seem contrary to all literary sense to repeat this entire
episode, I suspect that most of us have had the experience of starting
to read a paperback thriller which force of circumstance causes us to
put down after we have read only the opening chapters. Some days
later we try to pick up where we left off only to find that most of the
characters have become singularly anonymous. Frustrated at our
inability to recall who Chris, Ronnie, Yvonne and Mulligan are, we
hastily skim through the opening pages once more. Our memories
refreshed, we read on.

The convention of repeating the Exposition in sonata-form movements was established for a somewhat similar reason. It is a matter of
real importance to the composer that we should not only be able to
recognise themes when they reappear but also to be aware of the
proportions of the music, by which I mean the relative lengths of loud
or soft passages, whether themes are concise or expansive and where
notable changes of tone-colour occur. (More likely to be of
significance in an orchestral work than in a piano piece.) The further
advantage of this repetition, which is nowadays often dispensed with
since the works have become so familiar, is to whet the appetite for
what is to come. Having recognised the cadence which ends the
Exposition, Roger 'firmly closing the door', we are all the more eager
to know what happens next.

[1] 'I know I've been away from home for a bit', he said sternly, 'but
that's no reason for you to have been gadding around with Hamish.'

[2] 'But Roger darling, I haven't I swear.'

[3] 'Don't try and soft-soap me; you're lying and you know it.'

[4] 'How *can* you say that? It just isn't true...'

[5] 'We'll soon find out.'

[6] Grabbing her by the arm, Roger dragged her out into the street disregarding her shrill protestations which were quickly turning into alarm. Imperiously he hailed a passing taxi.

'Sloane Square', he commanded, 'and step on it, man.'

[7] Swiftly the taxi threaded its way through the back streets, so that anyone who didn't know London might well have lost all sense of direction. As they alighted from the cab, Stella turned pale.

[8] 'Hamish works here' she said, nodding towards an elegant doorway leading into an interior designer's showrooms.

'You're telling me' said Roger, the muscles of his jaw-line tense with anger.

'Roger, for God's sake, you're not going to make a scene. . . .'

[9] Without another word he pushed her roughly ahead of him into the chic interior. A bearded man rose startled from his desk.

'Hamish you bastard; I'll teach you to muck around with my girl!' Eyes blazing with anger, Roger stepped forward with the lightness of a born athlete and with two swift karate blows felled Hamish to the ground.

[10] Stella checked her instinctive impulse to rush to the aid of the stricken man.

[11] 'Roger, you really care don't you, you really care!'

'You bet I do' he replied.

[12] Tears in her eyes she reached out her hand, silently asking forgiveness.

Although not every Development section in a sonata is as action-packed as this epic scene, it is still possible to find a musical equivalent for almost every sentence. We must remember, though, that a sonata-form movement is not designed to tell a story. The Development, as the word implies, is mainly concerned with change; change of character, change of relationship, change of direction.

Sentence 1.   The Roger theme has been 'away from home for a bit', i.e. it has been heard in keys other than the 'home' key of the sonata; 'sternly' implies a new and more severe treatment of the theme, different from its jaunty presentation at the start of the movement. The mention of Hamish is the first inkling we have of a new theme which is destined to grow in importance.

Sentence 2.   Protesting and plaintive version of Stella's theme, cut short by

Sentence 3.   An angrier statement of the Roger theme.

Sentence 4.   More impassioned version of Sentence 2, higher in pitch and with more intense harmonies.

Sentence 5.   Abrupt allusion to Roger theme, now reduced to just a few notes.

Sentence 6.   In music this section would be called an Episode and would involve some aggressive passages derived from fragments of both Roger's and Stella's themes. The hailing of the taxi and the injunction to 'step on it' suggests a marked quickening of tempo and a strong forward impulse.

Sentence 7.   The swift passage through the back streets and the reference to losing all sense of direction becomes, in musical terms, a rapid sequence of modulations into unrelated keys (of which we will learn more later) and a consequent loss of touch with the 'home' key. Stella 'turning pale' is simply a pallid version of her theme.

Sentence 8.   The Hamish fragment that appeared early in the Development (Sentence 1) now establishes itself as a new tonal centre, which, since the man is clearly a cad, we may as well call the Sub-Dominant. The 'elegant doorway' is a rather stylish modulation into this new key. The Hamish theme, smooth and slightly cloying, is interleaved with repressed but tense allusions to the Roger theme ('jaw-muscles tense with anger') and further reference to the Stella theme as in Sentences 2 and 4.

Sentence 9.   This is the central climax of the movement, its physical violence conveyed in a torrent of octaves culminating in two massive chords (the karate blows) followed by a rapid descent to the bass of the keyboard. Over a long-held static bass note, Hamish flat on the floor, we find

Sentence 10.   fluttering allusions to the Stella theme, now some-
                 what disintegrated.

Sentence 11.   Warm emotional version of Stella theme which is
                 then combined briefly with a fragment of the Roger
                 theme ('You bet I do').

Sentence 12.   The quietest moment in the movement; slowing of
                 tempo; expressive harmony. A pause.

And so we come to the Recapitulation which I have described as a
re-assessment of the material in the light of experience gained during
the Development. The point is worth stressing since it is often implied
that it is no more than a boring convention which saves the composer
from the need to think of anything new. In fact, although the actual
notes of the First Subject may appear on paper to be identical to their
original form, *we who listen* have changed. The impact of those notes
at the start of the work, coming out of nothing with our emotions cold,
must be quite different at their reappearance since they have revealed
a potential of which we then had no knowledge. The fluctuations of
emotion in the music, the physical excitement of being present at the
performance have both played upon our own emotions. To revert to
my literary (!) parallel, we now 'know' Roger and Stella more intimately and have shared their drama. For reasons of plausibility, since
the time-scale of life is different from that of art, I have to cheat
slightly if we are to follow Roger's story to the end. In music one
cannot suggest a substantial jump in time except by embarking on a
completely new movement. In fiction it is a simple matter to say 'A
month later'. Here then is our Recapitulation.

[1] As Roger stepped out into the street he was reminded of the day when
he and Stella had quarrelled. He smiled to himself, remembering the
incident with Hamish. [2] If anything, his walk now was jauntier than
before as once again he entered the park; but this time there was no
need to cross over to the far side. [3] He circled round, his eyes on the
lookout for the slim elegant figure he so loved. [4] Ah, there she was,
observing her morning ritual of feeding the ornamental birds beside the
lake. She looked so contented, the sun picking out the highlights of her
flaxen hair, her skin golden in the morning light. [5] He approached her
softly, put a hand on her shoulder.
 [6] 'Roger darling,' she murmured, and then reached up and kissed him
tenderly.

'Coming home?' he asked.

'Yes', she said, 'I'm coming home.'

[7] Together they walked between the beds of flowers, fingers entwined. [8] When they reached his house he took the latch-key from his pocket, opened the door and led her inside. Lovingly they kissed as the door clicked shut. [9] They were home together.

Sentence 1.	Note that the introductory bars of Sentence 1 in the Exposition (see p. 38) are no longer required to establish the 'home' key; we can go straight into Roger's theme. His recollection of the day he and Stella quarrelled emphasises that his actions on this day are (so far) a repetition. The remembrance of the incident with Hamish is not meant to be done by any musical allusion; it is we in the audience who are sure still to have been influenced by the climax of the movement, not 'a month ago' but on the previous page.
Sentence 2.	Roger's theme with its accompaniment modified in such a way as to give it even more vitality.
Sentence 3.	A critical difference between Exposition and Development; instead of crossing the park to go to Stella's 'home', the Dominant, he 'circles round', i.e. stays within his own tonal centre, the Tonic. The journey, the Bridge Passage, is altered so that it does *not* modulate away from Roger's 'home' key.
Sentence 4.	This is a revised and somewhat altered lyrical passage, balancing Sentence 3 of the Exposition, but with a greater sense of anticipation of Stella's theme. The birds, sunlight etc. would find their musical equivalent in the use of trills or some shimmering figuration in the upper register of the keyboard.
Sentence 5.	A subtle modification of the end of Sentence 4 in the Exposition; instead of the swift arrival at the Stella theme we now have a gentler approach.
Sentence 6.	A repeat of the Second Subject, Stella's theme, but now in Roger's 'home' key, the Tonic instead of, as originally, her 'home' key, the Dominant.

Sentence 7.   The two themes combined in counterpoint with references to the decorative passage-work mentioned in Sentence 3 of the Exposition.

Sentence 8.   A lingering confirmation of Roger's 'home' key; 'the door clicked shut' could be a quiet version of the cadence originally found at 9, terminating the Exposition. Again it should be emphasised that this would now confirm the arrival at the Tonic rather than the Dominant key.

Sentence 9.   Soft ending, affirming not only the 'home' key but also the reconciliation of materials originally chosen for their contrast in character.

Sentences 8 and 9, clearly a rounding-off of the whole movement, would be called a *Coda* in musical terminology; a comparable but briefer passage at the end of the Exposition, assuming the composer decides to write one, would be a 'little coda' or *codetta*.

I think we may safely assume that this hypothetical 'Sonata' belongs to the Romantic period, partly because of the relatively lengthy Development section, but also because it is so concerned with the *transformation* of themes, a technique much favoured by such composers as Liszt, Tchaikovsky and Berlioz. A Mozart sonata would be far more compact, the general tone more refined. It was Beethoven who was largely responsible for enlarging the scope of a sonata-form movement. The difference is apparent at even the most mundane level if we compare the 21 pages of his first sonata, both influenced by and dedicated to Haydn, with the 52 pages of the so-called *'Hammerklavier'* sonata composed some twenty-three years later and bearing no resemblance to anything that had been written before, even by the composer himself.

Now, however fascinating the affair of Roger and Stella may have been, as soon as I suggested a possible musical equivalent it was impossible to avoid the use of the word 'key', or some phrase such as 'tonal centre'. We are accustomed to the idea of a composition being described as a 'Concerto in A minor', a 'Sonata in G major' or a 'Prelude in C sharp', but what significance does this have, and is it in any way important other than as a means of identification? It most certainly is, so much so that it deserves a chapter to itself.

5 __ The key question _____

'Can't you play something with a bit of tune in it?' calls an exasperated mother from the kitchen; 'I'm sick to death of hearing those wretched *scales*, up and down, up and down . . .'

Unfortunately the dreaded scales are part of the price every music student must pay if he or she wishes to acquire the basic technique of any instrument. Although we tend to think of them primarily as a physical exercise designed to increase the dexterity of the fingers, they have what is possibly a more significant value by giving the player a feeling for the musical concept known as Key. (The fact that the notes of the piano are also called keys is typical of the general confusion of musical nomenclature and should be disregarded.) A scale is simply a way of spelling out step by step those notes which collectively make up a key; thus the *scale* of A major might be described as a linear version of the *key* of A major. One would think therefore that any vertical combination of notes formed from the components of that scale would also be 'in' the key of A. Unhappily for those who would like music to be as simple as ABC this is not so, since no sequence of consecutive notes is unique to any one scale; there is always a certain amount of sharing to be taken into account. Those keys which have a number of notes in common are called 'related', and of these relationships the closest are between the first note of the scale, the Tonic, the fifth note of the scale, the Dominant, and the fourth note which, with uncharacteristic simplicity, is called the Sub-Dominant. Now when Roger crossed the park and entered Stella's apartment, the music *modulated* from the Tonic key to the Dominant key; this does not mean that the theme simply came to rest on the fifth note of Roger's scale but, more significantly, that Stella's scale *begins* on the fifth note of Roger's scale, thereby creating, if only temporarily, a new Tonic.

Modulation is the term used to describe the process of establishing a new key; Roger's journey across the park is therefore a Bridge Passage (a structural concept) which modulates (a functional concept) into a related key. The close relationship which exists between any Tonic and its Dominant and Sub-Dominant is easily explained: out of the seven notes that comprise a scale, six are shared. The scale of C major on the piano consists entirely of white notes; the scale of G (the Dominant) has one black note, as does the scale of F (the Sub-Dominant), but clearly the single black note is different in the two scales. (It is perhaps worth mentioning that because there are only seven notes we need only use the first seven letters of the alphabet, A–G. The Germans, for reasons too obscure to go into, also use H, but that really need not concern us at this stage.)

A simple, though musically illogical, way of expressing these relationships diagrammatically would be to assume that we should begin playing all three scales, C, G and F, from the same starting point, C.

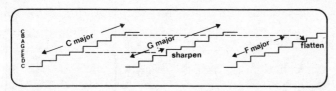

Fig. 9

To go from C major to G major it is necessary to raise, or *sharpen*, the fourth step of the scale; to go from C major to F major one must lower, or *flatten*, the seventh step. Consequently we say that G major has one 'sharp' (♯) while F major has one 'flat' (♭). Now a scale may have any number of flats or sharps between one and six; since C major has neither flats nor sharps, let us make it a central point from which the sharp keys rise and the flat keys fall. It seems a logical idea. (The number of sharps or flats required in any given key are shown as a little cluster at the beginning of each line of a piece of music; we can therefore tell at a glance that if a piece has a 'key signature' of three sharps, it will be in the key of A major whereas if it has five flats, it will be in D flat major. However, there is an alternative, as we shall see later.)

Shown vertically as in Fig. 10, it is easy to see which keys are closely related and which are remote from each other. Any note that you care to select as a Tonic will have its Dominant immediately above it and its Sub-Dominant immediately below it. This raises an interesting question: what is the Dominant of F sharp major or the Sub-Dominant of G flat? Is there a sort of outer rim beyond which we

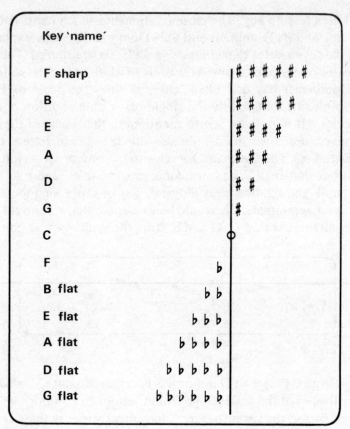

Fig. 10

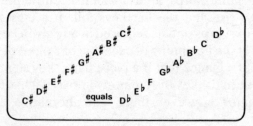

Fig. 11

cannot go? Observing that the distance between each named key in the left hand column is always a 5th (the distance from a Tonic to its Dominant or Sub-Dominant) the next logical step upwards in the column would bring us to C sharp, which would therefore have seven sharps in its key signature. This in fact is quite feasible but would give us a scale on the piano whose notes would be exactly the same as the scale of D flat, although more complex to the eye[1] (Fig. 11).

Five flats is obviously a simpler notation both to write and to read. If on the other hand we extend our column downwards, we arrive at a very curious-looking key, C flat major.

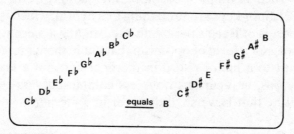

Fig. 12

This time it is five sharps that is the easier to take in. In appears then that there is a certain point where a change of identity needs to take place, C sharp major turning into a 'flat' key, C flat major turning into a 'sharp' key; yet this seems to occur at the point where on our

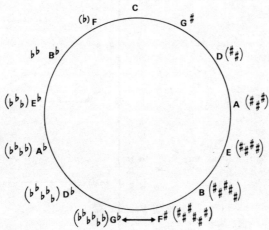

Fig. 13

---

[1] String players, with their ability to make very fine adjustments of intonation, could make a distinction between these two versions of what for pianists is the same scale. Scientifically speaking, C sharp and D flat are not identical but it would be quite impractical for a keyboard instrument to convey the very subtle difference (less than a quarter of a tone).

diagram the keys are most remote from each other, literally at opposite poles. Perhaps we should turn our vertical line into a circle so that instead of growing more distant from each other the keys with the most complex signatures converge (see Fig. 13).

So far we have concentrated entirely on *major* keys; how do we cope with a key such as B minor or, more interestingly as we shall see, A flat minor? Minor keys are something of a hybrid, which is the reason why composers of Bach's period disliked ending a piece with a minor chord. It was not a form of optimism that made them prefer to make a sudden shift to a major chord in the final bar, but a feeling that a minor key was, in a curious way, less committed, less certain of its identity. Why that is we shall discover in a moment.

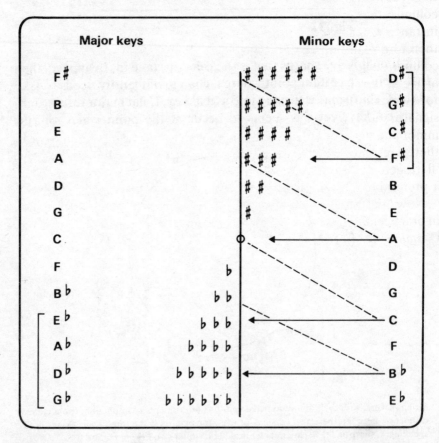

Fig. 14

There is one note in a minor scale that is unsure of itself for it exhibits a desire to sharpen in ascending passages and to flatten in descending ones. It is the seventh note of the scale, the so-called 'leading' note since it 'leads' us back to the Tonic in an upward progression. Because of this uncertainty the identity of this note is not shown in the key signature. What, then, are the key signatures of minor keys? Let us return to our vertical diagram which makes this particular point more clearly (see Fig. 14).

What in effect happens is that the vertical column of minor keys on the right corresponds exactly to the column of major keys on the left but shifted downwards ('flat'-wards) by three steps. Thus the key signature of F sharp minor is the same as that of A major; A minor corresponds to C major (in signature alone), B flat minor corresponds to D flat major and so on. Once we reach the lower end of the major column the change-of-identity law comes into operation. For instance we cannot go three steps downward from A flat major; we therefore read the second step down, G flat, as the *top* of the sharp column, its 'twin', F sharp, continue downwards a further step and arrive at the signature of B major, five sharps. A flat minor is therefore virtually always thought of as G sharp minor instead, since its key signature in flats would require seven flats. (Extend the idea to D flat minor and one would have a theoretical signature of eight flats; since there are only seven notes in the scale one note would have to be 'flattened' twice; undoubtedly the four sharps of C sharp minor offer a preferable alternative.)

Now I described minor scales as hybrids; let us see what this means in practice. Suppose we begin with a diagram to represent the scale of G *major*.

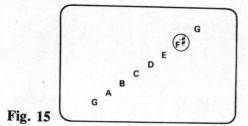

Fig. 15

To turn this into a scale of G minor we look back at Fig. 14 on p. 50. By making the sort of 'Knight's move' indicated, we discover that the signature is two flats, the same as that of B flat major. Apply these two flats to the proper notes and the scale would look like this:

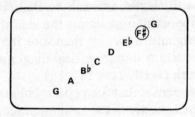

Fig. 16

At once the quandary becomes apparent; we now have a scale containing both flat and sharp notes. However we need not despair since if we come *down* the scale the F will probably become F *natural* (♮), a term which is used to cancel out either flat or sharp at will.

The ambivalence of the seventh note of the scale is not the only reason for the especial character of minor keys, although it is the largest contributory factor. We need to look further to realise its full implications. One crucial fact must be borne in mind: the chord based on the Dominant note of any key, the fifth note of the scale, is the same in both major and minor keys. Turn back to the circular diagram on p. 49. Suppose for the moment that I am a classical composer of the Haydn-Mozart era writing a sonata in C major. The music will largely inhabit the area shown in the arc F-C-G; excursions into more remote keys will be seen as adventures, disturbances of the norm. If, however, the sonata is in C minor, a greater portion of the circle will be easily accessible:

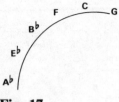

Fig. 17

G, being the Dominant, is common to both C major and C minor, but since the key signature of C minor corresponds to that of E flat, its immediate neighbours A flat and B flat are also easy of access. (Remember we are thinking in terms of the entire entities of A flat or

B flat, not just single notes.) We now see why minor keys are more volatile, more fluid than major keys. Although I have alternated rather freely between the words 'key' and 'scale' even though strictly speaking they are not interchangeable, I have so far avoided any description of the actual formation of scales. For the sake of simplicity the diagrams representing scales have shown them as a rising sequence of equal steps. This is not the case, as we shall discover when we look at the difference between tones and semitones. The narrowest interval on the piano keyboard, that between 'middle' C and the black note above it or the white note below it, is called a semitone. (There are smaller intervals, as we easily recognise when a young violinist plays out of tune; he is simply a microtone above or below the note he is trying to play.)

The interval made up of two consecutive semitones is called a tone; by varying the order in which tones and semitones follow each other it is possible to devise a wide variety of scales, but the formation of the major scale as used in Western music can be shown thus:

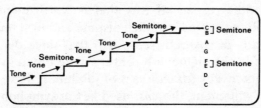

Fig. 18

the minor scale ascending would be:

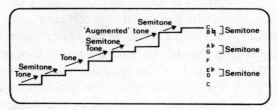

Fig. 19

the interval between A flat and B natural is wider than a tone and is described as 'augmented'. The minor scale descending would avoid this hazard:

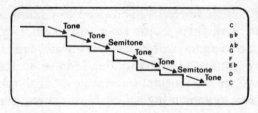

Fig. 20

A chromatic scale consists entirely of consecutive semitones.

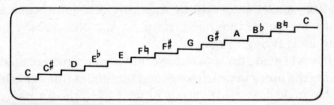

Fig. 21

There is another aspect of Key that is worth mentioning even though it is still the subject of much dispute amongst music scholars. We have already discovered (see p. 18) that since the most widely used trumpets in the eighteenth century were tuned in D, D major was the most likely key for choruses of jubilation. If we look for the reverse of this statement, the *least* used key in symphonic music is B flat minor because it is exceptionally awkward for the strings to play in tune. Now we have seen that the open strings of the violin are G, D, A and E, all 'sharp' keys. Perhaps because of this there seems to be a tendency for bright music to be in sharp keys and sombre music to be in flat keys – by implication *minor* flat keys. Thus keys such as G minor and C minor seem to have held a special emotional significance for Mozart, while A flat major seems to have been associated with an especially lyrical character in Beethoven's mind. C major is usually forthright in nature, while D major appears to have a pastoral feeling for a number of composers. The reason why this theory is open to dispute is that the actual *pitch* of the keys has changed over the centuries. We think of Beethoven's 'Moonlight' Sonata as being in C sharp minor, but he would actually have heard it at a considerably flatter pitch, much nearer to what we would call B minor. Get a musical friend to play its opening bars in B minor and see what a profound difference it makes.

During the nineteenth century modulation from one key to another became much more fluid until, in the hands of composers such as Liszt and Wagner, the whole framework of tonality, as the system of keys is called, began to crumble. In our own century some composers have consciously set out to destroy the entire concept, feeling that it was no longer capable of further development. However, the existence of the Harmonic Series (see p. 16, Fig. 2) is a fact of Nature, the first eleven components of the Series being agreeably concordant; they are so fundamental a part of musical sound that it smacks of perversity to disregard their implications.

Enough of theory – on with the music!

6__Variations on a theme _____

'Come along now, settle down – you've had all of twenty minutes; we're here to work, not natter away over cups of coffee . . .' Mr Roberts looks increasingly impatient as the last few stragglers hurry into the hall from the canteen down the corridor.

Terry dutifully produces a long sustained A for the orchestra to tune to and once again the hall is flooded with the strangely random cacophony that even the finest professional orchestra produces when tuning. After a moment or two a sort of silence descends.

'Turn to the slow movement will you,' says Mr Roberts. 'Cellos and violas, you have a real chance to show what you can do here so don't be shy. I know it looks a bit black later on, but just keep counting a nice steady three in your mind and it'll soon sort itself out.'

As he pauses, momentarily still before the first gentle stroke of the baton, one can sense the feeling of concentration that each of his young players brings to the task in hand. The relentless force of the first movement has effectively driven all outside thoughts from their minds; Beethoven has captured them, and as the graceful theme of the second movement casts its inevitable spell, even the players who for the moment are silent can be seen to be listening intently.

The number of movements in a symphony or sonata is a matter of choice for the composer; there is no absolute rule. There are even symphonies in one movement (Sibelius's Seventh comes to mind) but such specimens are rare and the pattern most generally adopted is to have four. Those with a sense of musical history tell us that this is because the symphony as a form developed from the Suite of contrasted dances with which composers of the late seventeenth century were expected to entertain their aristocratic or royal patrons. While this may be true from a genealogical viewpoint, I suspect that the real function of the movements is to display different aspects of the composer's skill. One might say that the first movement is likely to be the most intellectual in content, the second the most lyrical, the third the most light-hearted and the fourth the most aspiring; this at least is true of Beethoven, whose concept tended to establish a precedent for those who came after him. Certainly we can assume that the emotional content of a slow movement will be more consistent than that of a normal first movement since the emphasis will be more on feeling and less on argument. (By argument I mean the implied dispute that almost inevitably arises between First and Second Subjects in a sonata-form movement. Unless Roger and Stella have a quarrel, there is no conflict to resolve and hence no drama. This is particularly apparent in the first movement of Beethoven's Fifth Symphony in which the lyrical *Second* subject is persistently attacked from beneath by the menacing rhythmic pattern of the *First* subject.)

There is no reason why a slow movement should not also be in sonata form, but it is more likely that the composer will prefer a change of plan. In the movement that Mr Roberts has just begun to rehearse, Beethoven elected to write a particularly ingenious example of what is known as Variation Form. The earliest type of variations were simply decorative. First would come the theme, usually designed in such a way as to have a clearly recognisable outline and supported by relatively simple harmonies; a number of variations would then follow, depending on the resourcefulness of the composer. Since each variation would be the same length as the theme and share its harmonic structure, there was always a danger that sets of variations could be churned out according to a ready formula; on the other hand a great composer can display the most extraordinary ingenuity in extracting the utmost potential from initially unpromising material. I need hardly cite Elgar's Enigma Variations, Rakhmaninov's *Rhapsody on a Theme of Paganini* (actually variations) or Beethoven's monumental set of piano variations on the tritest of themes by Diabelli to make the point.

Since I am loth at this stage to introduce what would inevitably be a large number of increasingly complex music examples, let me resort

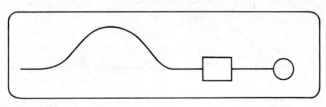

Fig. 22(a)

to crude graphics to illustrate the sort of treatment that might be applied to a theme. Suppose we represent the theme itself by the abstract pattern, Fig. 22(a); granted, it is not a thing of beauty, but it has its clearly recognisable features, a hump, a square and a circle. I would not dream of trying to 'translate' this into musical terms, but as soon as we start to think of it as a shape that can be given variation, the analogy can be pursued.

The first variation that would come to the mind of an eighteenth-century composer of Mozart's era would be to preserve the basic shape intact but to 'embroider' it, adding decorative but fundamentally superfluous notes.

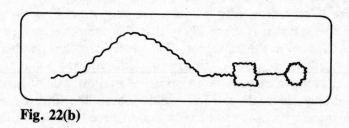

Fig. 22(b)

A likely alternative for the second variation would be to give the impression of doubling the speed by packing twice as many notes into each bar. This is difficult to convey visually since, as we have seen, when we look at a static image we are in control of Time and I cannot make you see an abstract shape more quickly. However, we can reduce it to half size:

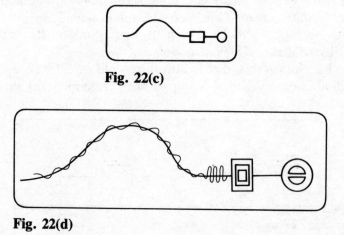

Fig. 22(c)

Fig. 22(d)

Composers such as Haydn, Mozart or Beethoven nearly always have one substantially lengthened variation, and it is here that the most elaborate decoration is likely to appear. (See Fig. 22(d))

If the theme is in a major key, one variation will almost certainly be in the minor; since this means flattening the 3rd and 6th notes of the key and 'darkening' the harmony, I will flatten the hump and shade in the spaced areas.

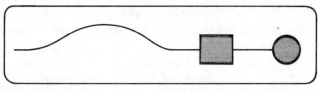

Fig. 22(e)

The final variation will probably turn out to be more expansive, developing the main features and even breaking out quite freely towards the end.

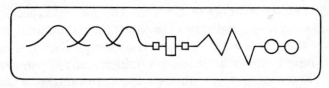

Fig. 22(f)

However, the relationship to the theme will still be apparent to the attentive ear as it is here to the perceptive eye.

In the set of variations which constitute the slow movement of Beethoven's Fifth Symphony, the composer has devised an altogether more elaborate plan. The choice of tonality is interesting for the main theme of the movement is in A flat major, a close 'relative' of C minor (the key of the first movement) because it has only one more flat in its key signature. But there is an important subsidiary theme, quite different in character, which habitually appears in C *major*, a key that contradicts all the vital characteristics of A flat major but which at least shares a common root with C minor. (It also anticipates the key of the finale, but that is possibly of no great significance.)

The movement begins with the simplest imaginable presentation of the theme, violas and cellos gently playing in unison, while the double basses sketch in a few notes in support, their strings being plucked rather than bowed. (It is worth mentioning that Beethoven frequently combines violas and cellos when a theme of importance appears in their register, probably because in his experience their numbers were always sparse in comparison to the violins.) The last four notes of the opening phrases are affirmed warmly by the full string section. It is a fragment that proves to be irresistible, so much so that the choir of woodwind instruments takes it over, extending it into a lyrical phrase of great beauty. It is then the turn of the strings to elaborate it still more affectionately. The section is concluded quite positively with four chords of A flat major. We are fully justified in thinking that this is the end of the theme and that the first variation is imminent. In fact he has a surprise for us, since clarinets and bassoons introduce what appears to be a new theme, even though it is still in the same gentle mood. Its entry seems to be premature, for after only two brief phrases an element of doubt creeps in, with the violins posing a sort of musical question-mark. 'Do you really mean this?' they seem to be asking. With a slam of his fist on the table, Beethoven shouts 'Yes!' and the music breaks through into the quite unexpected key of C major. Horns, trumpets and timpani ram the point home. The subsidiary theme, so gentle at its first appearance on clarinets and bassoon, now assumes a ferociously military air; the music seems confident of triumph. Again, though, the violins interrupt with their soft question, 'Did you mean that?' and this time there is no answer, only a retreat into the shadows. It is a passage full of mystery, but which leads us by a back-door route back to the home key of A flat.

It is at this point that Beethoven introduces Variation 1 on the main theme. It is easily recognisable since, like the theme, it is given to violas and cellos in unison. Furthermore it is a classic example of the 'embroidered' type of variation shown in Fig. 22(b). As before, the final phrase is confirmed by the violins, blessed by the woodwind and caressed by the strings. Again four repeated chords of A flat major terminate the section.

Beethoven now embarks on a virtual repetition of the whole of the subsidiary section. Only different in detail, it offers the same questionings, the same explosion into C major, the same military triumph dissolving into mystery. The same devious route leads us back to A flat major and, in due course, Variation 2 on the main theme. This too proves to comply with a formula, the one of giving an impression of increased speed by packing more notes into each bar. Whereas in Variation 1 the violas and cellos were given six notes to play in each bar they now have twelve. (The way this is written, ♫♫♫♫♫♫, caused Mr Roberts's remark about it looking 'a bit black' later on.) The violins, seemingly eager to show that they are just as capable, repeat this variation, whereupon, to the accompaniment of some rather cheerful repeated chords in the woodwind and brass, the cellos are joined by some uncharacteristically agile double basses in what might be called a variation on a variation. Two loud ascending scales in the Dominant key of E flat put a stop to all this and the music literally comes to a halt. Very quietly the strings begin to mark time; clarinet, bassoon and then the upper woodwind produce a beautifully free derivation of the main theme, their liquid tones making a lovely contrast to the darker sonorities which have tended to colour the movement. Suddenly a call to action from the horns reintroduces the subsidiary theme in a truly majestic guise. Once again, though, the sounds fade away as if uncertain which course to take. A strange murmuring figure in the strings hovers almost inaudibly on the chord of E flat, the Dominant of the 'home' key. We sense that this must surely lead us back to A flat major, but the long postponement suggests that Beethoven has other plans. With one of the most subtle inventions of the entire movement he moves into A flat *minor*. Flute, clarinet and bassoon in unison introduce a wholly new variant on the theme, turning into quite unexpected directions. A few fragmentary rising scales scattered across the orchestra seem designed to erase this new element and, sure enough, the main theme makes a triumphant reappearance, really asserting itself for the first time with violins and wind singing out the tune over a throbbing accompaniment. Massive rising scales terminate this section, leaving the woodwind alone to add their benediction which, as before, is echoed by the strings.

A slight increase in tempo tells us that we have arrived at the Coda, a final section whose function is to round things off satisfactorily. A rather plaintive bassoon offers a relevant comment, to which violas and cellos give their muttered approval. Three rising phrases in the violins suggest that the end is in sight, but again Beethoven cannot resist the desire to savour once more the lovely woodwind phrase that now appears for the fourth time. The strings cap it with a profoundly expressive gesture, the most openly emotional moment of the whole movement. Clarinets and bassoons seem to fuse elements of the two predominating themes, whereupon Beethoven decides that it is time to close the door, which he does with some increasingly emphatic repetitions of the chord of A flat. This time he is 'home' to stay.

Had I attempted to describe the first movement in this sort of detail, it would have seemed intolerably wearisome since, despite its tremendous dynamism, it is composed of exceptionally short phrases. It is these that give the music such urgency. In the slow movement the time-scale is quite different, the first theme alone being longer than any single phrase in the opening movement. Needless to say, not all slow movements are in variation form; in Beethoven's 'Eroica' Symphony we find a Funeral March, while the slow movements of Mozart's piano concertos are virtually operatic arias in which the piano stands in for the absent soprano. In Beethoven's 'Moonlight' Sonata the slow movement comes first; in Tchaikowsky's 'Pathétique', the Sixth, it comes at the end. Composers do not abide by rules unless they are self-imposed. What is important is that the overall structure of the movement should be satisfying.[1] In this movement Beethoven with great ingenuity combines strictly classical variations with one aspect of sonata form – the essential contrast between the first and second subject. In doing so he devised a plan that is more than just unusual; the great authority on Beethoven, Sir Donald Tovey, went so far as to call it unique. The casual listener has no idea of this; he hears an attractive tune with, at times, some loud interruptions of a vaguely martial kind; he is aware that some passages sound mysterious while others seem to be elaborately decorated; he will even accept that it is 'Great Music' since it appears to be generally agreed that if it is by Beethoven it must be Good. But fully to appreciate its qualities demands much more than casual listening, and it is perhaps pertinent to reveal that Beethoven's original plan for the movement was for it to be a traditional Minuet, though with the same subsidiary theme as a contrasting central section. His total rejection of this idea shows how conscious he was of the boldness of his break with convention, a boldness which familiarity should not allow us to forget.

---

[1] In the first movement the Exposition is 124 bars long, the Development 123 bars, the Recapitulation 126 and the Coda 129!

7 __ All in jest

As though from the very depths, cellos and basses make their almost inaudible ascent through the opening phrase; the upper strings, flecked with just a touch of woodwind, give a gentle but uncertain response, ending on a pause. Again the cellos and basses climb out of the darkness, again comes the hesitant reply. The orchestra has begun the third movement, the so-called *Scherzo*. Since the word literally means a jest it could hardly be less suitable. This music is ghostly, mysterious, at times strident, but it is certainly no joke. Like the slow movement that precedes it, it is a totally original invention, confounding all expectation, more of an improvisation for orchestra than a traditionally cheerful dance movement. Indeed this tentative opening is just the sort of thing one might expect from a pianist who, seated at the keyboard without any great conviction about what he is going to play, tries out a couple of phrases to see if they are worth pursuing.

The traditional third movement of a four-movement symphony is perhaps the best evidence that the symphony as a form derives from a dance suite, since it continued to be called a Minuet or *Menuetto* long after both its tempo and its mood had ceased to have any practical application in the ballroom. Since contrast is the breath of life in music, it was thought necessary to have a central section consisting of quite different material, usually rather more lightly scored. The first part would then be played again in a shortened version, abbreviated by the simple method of *not* repeating sections which initially were played twice. The central section (with no perceptible logic) was habitually called the *Trio*, though it is hardly ever played by only three instruments, which such a title would suggest. I have never seen a satisfactory explanation for its curious name. Admittedly in Bach's day there were occasions when the Trio was indeed scored for three instruments, but it was by no means a generally accepted convention and certainly not enough to justify perpetuating the term in symphonic works.

The minuet as a dance first appeared in the French courts around 1650; in those days it was quite a stately affair whose formality was emphasised by its rigid structure of two sections of similar length, usually 16 bars, each of which was repeated. Gradually over the years its pulse quickened; Haydn in particular became impatient with the formula, not only increasing the tempo but releasing the music from its formal straitjacket by introducing asymmetrical lengths of phrase, as for instance when he follows a four-bar phrase with one of six bars. The sum total of ten instead of the conventional eight catches the listener unawares and would certainly have upset anyone trying to dance the usual pattern of steps to it.

Since Beethoven studied with Haydn, it is not surprising that he profited by his teacher's example, and the so-called Menuetto of his First Symphony (1800) fairly sizzles along. By the time he came to write his Second Symphony (1803) Beethoven realised the absurdity of calling a movement a Minuet when it was obviously no such thing; he therefore adopted the Italian word *Scherzo* to show that if nothing else it was meant to be fun. (Curiously enough he re-adopted the old term in his Fourth Symphony, though the music is so explosive in character that one can only assume that to call it a Menuetto appealed to his sardonic sense of humour.)

In the case of the Fifth Symphony Beethoven jettisoned the idea of a title altogether, simply heading the movement with the terse instruction *Allegro*, meaning 'quick'. Despite this the music doesn't give the impression of being fast, partly because of the strange hesitant character of the opening pages. It is a curious feature of this symphony, whose first movement is so relentless in its drive, that in both of the central movements we find a tendency for the music to halt in its tracks, as if uncertain of its course. We have already seen how in the slow movement the martial-sounding theme loses all confidence; here, at the start of the scherzo, even the initial confidence is not there to lose. Suddenly, as if saying to himself the period equivalent of 'Snap out of it!' Beethoven introduces a powerful theme on the horns, accompanied by emphatic chords from the strings. It is a theme that cannot fail to make its mark, beginning as it does with twelve repetitions of the same note in RA-ta-ta-TAT rhythm. It is taken up almost ferociously by the full wind and strings, giving the impression that nothing could stand in its way. This is just where we are wrong for, as in the slow movement, the very themes which seem most confident are the ones that soon disintegrate. The sound dies away, and again cellos and basses offer their mysterious opening phrase, now in the clearly alien key of B flat minor. As before, the quiet response from strings and wind comes to a halt. Yet again the mysterious phrase rises out of the gloom; it is like a sinister magician conjuring some evil spell. But this time the music gains momentum, growing in intensity until the horn theme reappears, its rhythm hammered out even more insistently than before. As the movement progresses, the span of the phrases becomes longer and longer, and though there are still moments of doubt, a long-drawn-out *crescendo* carries us along to what seems to be the inevitable powerful closing cadence. Once again it is unsafe to make assumptions since the last four bars are suddenly hushed.

At this point Beethoven draws a double bar-line across the page, and were the movement to behave at all in an orthodox way, the entire first part would be repeated. Instead, he pushes on into what for want of a better term would, in an O-level paper, be described as the Trio. I say 'for want of a better term' since there is actually no term that would accurately describe this stroke of imaginative genius.

Cellos and basses lead off with the utmost confidence. Gone is the mystery, gone the doubts and hesitations. The mood is brisk and forthright and, as if to reassure us that sanity has been restored at last, the music is laid out as a fugue. This is more alarming to the uninitiated listener than it need be. At this stage all we need to know is that the cellos present the bustling theme in the Tonic (C major), the violas copy it in the Dominant, (G) second violins duly come in with the same theme in the Tonic and first violins top the lot in the Dominant. (In fact they are so eager to come in that their entry seems a bit premature.) It's all suspiciously neat and tidy and Beethoven soon reveals that it is what we call a 'send-up', a caricature of academicism. Having convinced us that it's a fugue, or more properly – since it's so short – a 'little' fugue or *Fughetta*, it then repeats itself, something no respectable fugue would ever do. This apparently bewilders the orchestra. Everyone stops. Cellos and basses make two abortive attempts to get going again and then, after some academic note-spinning, do finally manage to start the fugue once more, a feat which is so enthusiastically greeted by the wind and brass that the music stops being a fugue and becomes a country dance instead. Beethoven then repeats his joke with the cellos and basses; but just when we assume that this is a mere repetition of what has gone before, he surprises us by staying on tiptoe, thinning out the texture

until virtually nothing is left save a few isolated notes plucked somewhat incredulously by the lower strings.

Now if we are to take the word *Scherzo* at its face value as a jest,
there can be no doubt where the joke lies. It is in this central section
whose purpose is clearly humorous. One could say with some
justification that in this amazingly original movement the Scherzo is
put in the middle, where the Trio would normally be, and that it is
flanked on both sides by what I have described as 'an improvisation
for orchestra'. The improvisatory nature of the music is underlined by
what happens next. The very opening phrase reappears, and every
listener in Beethoven's time would have felt reassured that here, at
least, orthodox procedures would be observed. Obviously Beethoven
has gone back to Square One and will repeat the whole of the first part
with suitable abbreviations.

At the risk of labouring the point I must stress that we cannot fully
appreciate this music simply by hearing the sound it makes. Throughout the movement Beethoven is playing games with us, suggesting
that he is going to do one thing and then doing something else.
The surprises are not merely aural; they are structural, rather as
though we were to find a thatched roof over the vestry of a Norman
church. The third section of this movement contains the biggest
surprise of all.

Beginning with all the appearance of a normal reprise, it turns into
something completely unexpected. As though in a whisper, the
clarinets play what was once the strident horn theme. It is like a
children's game in which, having been exhorted not to wake Gran-
dad, they continue to play, exaggerating the near silence with which
they creep around the room. At any moment, one feels, someone will
knock something over. For some time the music continues as quietly
as possible, its latent energy unnaturally suppressed. Suddenly – and
it is one of the most unforgettable moments in the Symphony – the
strings freeze as they hear the distant beat of a drum. RA-ta-ta-TAT,
RA-ta-ta-TAT it taps out, reminding us of the horn theme. Soon the
beat becomes a steady pulsation. Weirdly distorted fragments of the
initial theme rise uncertainly in the violins. Gradually, driven on by
the insistent throb of the drum, their phrases climb higher, reaching
towards the light. It is like one of those nature films in which we see a
month's growth of a plant compressed into the span of thirty seconds.
At the peak of the phrase a high chord on strings and wind shimmers
and glows like a dazzling gleam of sunlight bursting through the

morning haze. Without further ado we are pitched into the finale.

It may seem a little perverse on my part to have chosen so atypical a movement to illustrate what a scherzo is like. However, one could scarcely find a better way of showing the freedom with which great composers treat established forms. The rules, such as they are, are there to be broken, and perhaps the only symphonies which behave with absolute propriety are those written to satisfy the requirements of examiners at a university.

Are the rules worth knowing then? Indeed yes, since one can only appreciate the inspired departure from orthodoxy if one is aware of what orthodoxy dictates. It is amazing how easily the conservative musical mind is disturbed. Cherubini was much criticised for including a single funereal note on a gong in his Requiem; César Franck was informed that no symphony could properly have a cor anglais (a sort of bass oboe) in it. When Tchaikovsky incorporated a delicious waltz into his Fifth Symphony he upset numerous critics, even though all he was doing was to find a contemporary equivalent to the long outmoded minuet. As we continue to explore music we must be ever more astonished at its variety; but we sometimes forget that even the most familiar classical work was once a 'modern' piece. We all now accept that Beethoven's Fifth Symphony is a masterpiece, yet at the first rehearsal it ever had in London, in 1816, the orchestra laughed out loud at the opening, refusing to take it seriously. Their attitude was not discouraged by the conductor who declared the work to be rubbish. (In all fairness he recanted some years later and acknowledged it to be one of the greatest compositions he had ever heard.) It appears that 'our' rehearsal has ground to a halt; there is some talk of missing players. At *this* stage? What can have gone wrong?

8 _Last movements _____

'Where are my trombones?' calls Mr Roberts.

'They're out at the back, Sir', comes an anonymous reply from someone in the wind section.

'Well, somebody go and fetch them; I told them they could come late but that doesn't mean missing their cue altogether.'

Footsteps can be heard hurrying across the curtained-off stage in search of the missing brass players.

'Is Evelyn here?'

A girl with dark hair cut in a boyish style holds up her hand and waves a piccolo to catch the conductor's eye.

'That's fine; sorry you've had to wait so long but that's Beethoven's fault, not mine.'

'What about the contra-bassoon, Sir?' says a studious-looking boy in the front desk of the cellos, perhaps eager to show that he knows the score.

'Oh, Mr MacWhinnie will be coming in to play that on the day. I don't think we need bother him at this stage.'

Mr MacWhinnie is the peripatetic teacher of woodwind, one of those amazingly versatile players who seem to be able to play any wind instrument with enviable ease. An ex-military bandsman, his greatest delight is to coach a group of young wind players, passing on an enthusiasm that shows no sign of waning with the years. Proud owner of a large collection of wind instruments, he is the only person in the district likely to possess anything as exotic as the contra-bassoon that Beethoven asks for in the final movement. Deepest-voiced of all the wind family, its existence is hardly recognised by the ordinary music lover, except when its fruity lower notes elicit suppressed mirth during Dukas' *The Sorcerer's Apprentice.*

The scraping of chairs and the noisy collapse of a music stand at the back of the orchestra signal the arrival of the errant trombonists. With a cheerful 'Sorry Sir' and a few honks reminiscent of an old-style taxi the three of them settle down, oblivious of the whispered sarcasm of their immediate neighbours.

dies away, and again cellos and basses offer their mysterious opening phrase, now in the clearly alien key of B flat minor. As before, the quiet response from strings and wind comes to a halt. Yet again the mysterious phrase rises out of the gloom; it is like a sinister magician conjuring some evil spell. But this time the music gains momentum, growing in intensity until the horn theme reappears, its rhythm hammered out even more insistently than before. As the movement progresses, the span of the phrases becomes longer and longer, and though there are still moments of doubt, a long-drawn-out *crescendo* carries us along to what seems to be the inevitable powerful closing cadence. Once again it is unsafe to make assumptions since the last four bars are suddenly hushed.

At this point Beethoven draws a double bar-line across the page, and were the movement to behave at all in an orthodox way, the entire first part would be repeated. Instead, he pushes on into what for want of a better term would, in an O-level paper, be described as the Trio. I say 'for want of a better term' since there is actually no term that would accurately describe this stroke of imaginative genius.

Cellos and basses lead off with the utmost confidence. Gone is the mystery, gone the doubts and hesitations. The mood is brisk and forthright and, as if to reassure us that sanity has been restored at last, the music is laid out as a fugue. This is more alarming to the uninitiated listener than it need be. At this stage all we need to know is that the cellos present the bustling theme in the Tonic (C major), the violas copy it in the Dominant, (G) second violins duly come in with the same theme in the Tonic and first violins top the lot in the Dominant. (In fact they are so eager to come in that their entry seems a bit premature.) It's all suspiciously neat and tidy and Beethoven soon reveals that it is what we call a 'send-up', a caricature of academicism. Having convinced us that it's a fugue, or more properly – since it's so short – a 'little' fugue or *Fughetta*, it then repeats itself, something no respectable fugue would ever do. This apparently bewilders the orchestra. Everyone stops. Cellos and basses make two abortive attempts to get going again and then, after some academic note-spinning, do finally manage to start the fugue once more, a feat which is so enthusiastically greeted by the wind and brass that the music stops being a fugue and becomes a country dance instead. Beethoven then repeats his joke with the cellos and basses; but just when we assume that this is a mere repetition of what has gone before, he surprises us by staying on tiptoe, thinning out the texture

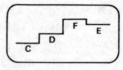

Fig. 23(a)

This has a slightly waggish tail which does not need to be quoted. In a matter of seconds it leads to the first surprise of the movement, a strongly reinforced statement of Theme 1 that suggests a hero wielding his sword in defence of a frightened maiden. (As in so much of Mozart's music, one feels that the operatic stage is only just around the corner.) Theme 2, which shortly follows, is basically a decorated descending scale whose first note is repeated three times in a martial rhythm

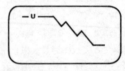

Fig. 23(b)

It excites a considerable amount of activity in the orchestra with further scales scampering here and there, leading to a very positive halt. There is a tiny silence (we are still less than a minute into the movement) out of which emerges, or so it seems, Theme 1 on second violins alone. However, the last note has been cut off and replaced by a little dancing figure picked out note by note like pinpoints of light. This three-notes-plus-a-dance is treated fugally, that is to say with a series of ingeniously overlapping entries. (See Fig. 23(c))

As though too impatient to allow this procedure to continue much longer, horns and trumpets come blaring in accompanied by a cannon-shot from the timpani. At once the character of the preceding three-note theme (reduced from four remember) is changed; it becomes positive to the point of aggression. Furthermore it has a sting in its tail, an abrupt little rising phrase with a little stabbing trill on the fourth note: (Fig. 23(d))

This too is treated to some overlapping as though violins and cellos literally 'can't get together'.

The tension is screwed up more tightly, the breaking-point coming with the scale theme (Fig. 23(b)) which, like the 'sting' section

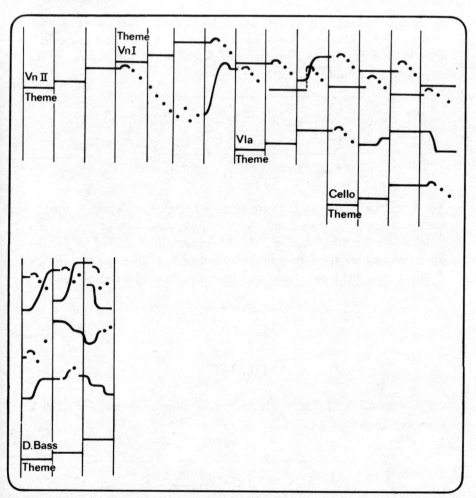

Fig. 23(c)

Fig. 23(d)

immediately before it, shows upper and lower strings chasing each other. Again there is a tiny silence; we have reached the open door that leads into the Dominant key. A theme of the utmost grace appears, a veritable Princess:

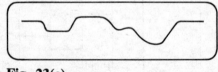

Fig. 23(e)

The previously almost ferocious scale theme (23b) now converts itself into the Princess's page-boy, skipping nimbly after her (a solo flute) while the 'sting' theme (23d) becomes a little chuckle of laughter on two bassoons. We should also notice a seemingly insignificant detail, four specks like raindrops, usually played by the oboes:

Fig. 23(f)

These four ideas, 'Princess', 'raindrops', 'sting' and 'scale' interlock most ingeniously.

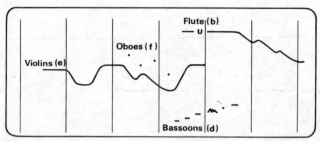

Fig. 23(g)

Mozart plays with these ideas delightfully, flutes and bassoons tossing the 'sting' theme to each other while the violins do a little quiet scale practice in the background. Suddenly the mood changes quite violently; just as the very opening theme of four notes had suffered an amputation, so now the Princess theme loses its elegant train. It too is reduced to three notes and subjected to heated argument.

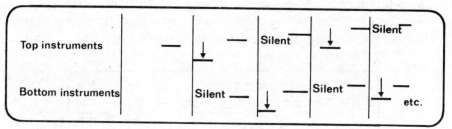

Fig. 23(h)

This is now developed into four-part counterpoint, the theme over-lapping itself at four different levels: the 'train' is restored, but changed from satin to cord, its once smooth lines now ruffled into abrupt staccato.

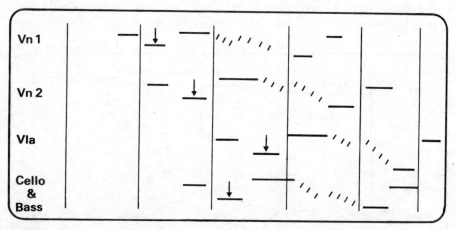

Fig. 23(i)

This development not unnaturally leads to considerable turbulence; it may be in the learned style but it certainly is not lacking in passion. To enumerate all the marvels of this movement would be unnecessarily wearisome; time after time the various components are played off against each other while also being subjected to subtle changes – a sudden twist into a minor key or a reversal of direction. The supreme moment comes towards the end of the movement. To the blare of horns and trumpets and the thud of the drum is added the scale theme, now exploding outwards in opposite directions. Again we find a tiny silence, the pause that always heightens expectancy; with an expressive melancholy quite new to the movement the strings introduce an interlocking version of Theme 1, now turned upside down.

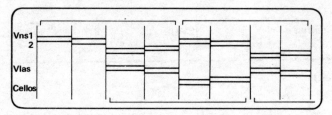

Fig. 23(j)

There follows a classic instance of sheer genius in the handling of counterpoint; it is a section that I call 'curtain-calls' in which all five of the themes quoted are interwoven, the 'characters' taking a final bow in a happy group.

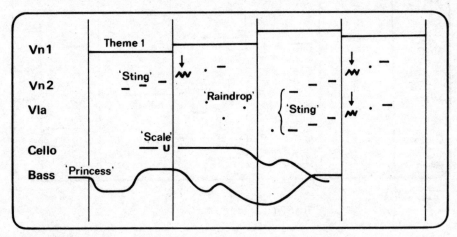

Fig. 23(k)

Only four bars are depicted here but Mozart actually juggles with these fragments for some thirty bars in all with the themes constantly switching positions. To what degree this was contrived in advance it would be hard to say; one certainly does not start work on a movement by knitting together a complex fabric of ideas and then pulling them apart. I suspect that Mozart intuitively produced fragments that would fit together but was himself surprised and delighted when he found how neatly it worked out; there is an air of discovery in the way the fusion of ideas materialises.

A popular form for a finale, less intellectually challenging than the concentrated brilliance we find in the 'Jupiter', is the *Rondo*. It is a sort of musical equivalent to a multi-decker sandwich in which the recurring theme is comparable to the bread while the intervening 'episodes' correspond to the various different fillings. The movement will begin with the main theme which is likely to be more song-like than the first subject of a sonata-form movement would be, largely because the composer is anxious that we should be able to recognise it easily on the several occasions that it is due to return. Once the Rondo-theme has run its course, an episode will follow, most probably in a closely related key such as the Dominant.

The episode will duly give way to the Rondo-theme which, to aid recognition still further, will almost certainly reappear in the 'home' key. Once again we embark on a journey into new material, this time into another related key, perhaps the sub-dominant or maybe the relative minor (see p. 50). Such an excursion would provide the opportunity for a change of mood which the ultimate return to the Rondo-theme would effectively dispel. If the composer feels that a Rondo is by its very nature too discursive for his purpose, he may well decide to reinforce its structure by introducing some of the disciplines of sonata form, though the distinction between a Rondo and a Sonata-form Rondo is something that is of greater concern to candidates for a musical diploma than to the ordinary listener.

There are also some notable examples of last movements in Variation form; the finale of Beethoven's 'Eroica' Symphony (No. 3) immediately comes to mind, while even the choral section of his Ninth Symphony is, despite its hugely complex plan, a set of variations. Brahms, in his Fourth Symphony, uses a particularly strict form of variation in which the essential bone-structure, a mere eight bars long, is retained no less than thirty times before at last breaking free. One might suppose the effect of such repetition to become extremely monotonous, but Brahms is so skilful in inventing new superstructures to mount on the recurring framework that we cannot fail to be amazed at the sheer ingenuity of it.

The finale of Beethoven's Fifth Symphony, which as we have seen requires the addition of piccolo, contra-bassoon and three trombones to enhance its impact, is an elaborate example of a sonata-form movement even though at first it appears as if it is going to be a triumphal march. However, its most striking moment shows a marvellously imaginative departure from the normal progress of the form for, at the very climax of the Development, the music is suddenly interrupted by the entrance of a ghost. The strident horn theme from the third movement reappears, reduced to bare bones; it is totally unexpected and never fails to capture the listener's imagination as an event of peculiar importance. So far as I know there is only one precedent, and that in a somewhat obscure symphony by Haydn, No. 46 in B major, which presumably Beethoven had discussed with his master at some time. Later such transpositions from one movement to another were to become a popular device of Romantic composers such as Liszt, Tchaikovsky and Berlioz. In the latter's truly Fantastic Symphony the so-called 'motto' theme appears in every one of its five movements, even though at times one gets the impression that it has been added as an afterthought.

Another clearly recognisable feature of the finale of Beethoven's Fifth Symphony is the Coda which develops into a headlong gallop for the finishing line. The very end of the symphony has been much caricatured for its over-emphatic insistence on the tonic chord of C major, to which Beethoven resolutely sticks for 29 bars; clearly he must have felt that after so adventurous a musical journey the arrival 'home' should be hailed with special enthusiasm. In an age when tonality, the identity of key, played so important a role in the composer's mind, the establishment of the tonic at the beginning and end of a work was felt to be essential; this was especially true in the larger musical structures where certain points of reference were always made clear, the end of the Exposition establishing the Dominant key, the journeys into alien territory in the Development, the positive reaffirmation of the Tonic at the start of Recapitulation, its confirmation in the closing bars. These were not mere academic conventions but what might be termed navigational aids for the listener, designed to give recognisable landmarks to help him find his bearings. As the margins of tonality gradually became less clearly defined, a procedure initiated by Beethoven and consummated by Wagner, these classic features began to crumble. Based as it was on the significance of key-relationships, even the concept of sonata form began to lose its appeal for composers, and it is worth pointing out that whereas Beethoven wrote 32 piano sonatas, Liszt, Chopin and Schumann barely produced seven between them. As the turbulent waters of Romanticism flooded the Classical temples, descriptive music became the new fashion. Inspiration came from sources outside music, from literature, from painting, from myth and legend. New types of music appeared with titles unknown in the eighteenth century – Ballade, Intermezzo, Capriccio, Rhapsody, Nocturne or Symphonic Poem. But although the full flood of Romanticism did not appear until after his death, Beethoven must be held largely responsible for opening the flood gates. Initially he accepted his inheritance from Haydn and Mozart but, perhaps aided by the isolation imposed by his deafness, he was to revolutionise the concept of music's potential, stretching the traditional classical restraints of form until they were near to breaking-point. And break they did, as his late string quartets clearly show. Their form is far from chaotic; he was too great a composer for that. But their frequent changes of direction, fluctuations of tempo and startling modulations show his determination to break away from past conventions. The formula had become too pat for so restless an intellect. We who listen need to be aware of such things; we need to cultivate a historic sense, not by knowing the exact date a work was written, but by being able to place it in the continuing creative flow. We need to know just when a composer is stepping beyond the boundaries set by contemporary taste and to what extent he is challenging his audience. The easiest successes are scored by those who make the least demands; the desire to come to terms with a true masterpiece presupposes that we are willing to make some effort ourselves, for we are not just hearing *sounds*; we are hearing *thoughts* expressed in sound. Few of us fail to respond to the openly emotional aspect of music, the clamour of the brass, the surge of strings, the force of percussion; but to the composer emotion is often an almost accidental feature, a fleeting moment in a structure where contrast of patterns, changes of direction or the transformation of themes seem of far greater importance. Even a composer as openly romantic as Liszt took enormous pains to devise a totally original and yet structurally convincing design for his great piano sonata, a single movement that takes nearly half an hour to play. The whole work is built on no more than five themes, most of them terse in the extreme. Yet in the course of the work these themes undergo extraordinary changes of character. Can one seriously contend that it was a matter of indifference to the composer whether such changes were comprehended or not? Of course we can't; it is vital to our appreciation of such a work that we should follow every change of mood, not just as emotional stimuli but as the evolution of ideas. Since composers are specialists in a highly specialised language, the least we can do is to give them our full attention.

Part Two

9 _Partnerships _____

The rehearsal is over. Mr Roberts, looking as though he has just had a pretty good work-out in the gym, is for the moment surrounded by half a dozen or more children asking questions, to most of which, had they been listening properly, he has already given the answers.

'Yes, Pam, it *will* be white blouses and black skirts on the night; have I ever asked you to wear anything different? What is it Nigel? One of the keys is sticking on your clarinet? Well, take it along to Mr MacWhinnie; he'll fix it for you I'm sure.' Seeing some of his players already elbowing their way through the swing doors, he suddenly adopts his loudest parade-ground voice. 'If anyone's thinking of taking a part home to practise, you *must* see Miss Stebbing first and sign for it: got that?'

Miss Stebbing, threading her way awkwardly through a maze of chairs and stands, has her arms heavily laden with the parts she has gathered up so far. With a loud thud she deposits them on the stage and picks up a clip-board, string and pencil attached. A few conscientious souls duly sign their names, resolving to do battle with Beethoven in the privacy of their homes. As the hall empties, Mr Roberts gathers up score and batons and slumps into a chair in the front row.

'I'm knackered,' he announces to the world at large, and proceeds to wipe the sweat off his brow with a handkerchief already well-moistened from his labours.

Throughout the rehearsal a man has been sitting alone in the main body of the hall, inevitably bored at times, but for the most part clearly fascinated by this introduction to an aspect of school life of which he had previously been unaware. With an almost deferential air he approaches the conductor.

'Might I have a word – that's if you're not worn out . . .'

'But of course; what can I do for you?' With a gesture Mr Roberts invites the stranger to sit beside him. 'Forgive me for not standing up but I feel as though I've been on my feet for hours; it's quite a hard slog that symphony you know, especially at this stage when the kids need driving along.'

'I can imagine . . . Still, it must be good exercise waving your arms about like that; no wonder conductors live to a great age. By the way, my name's Malcolm; my nephew, young Jeremy Warrilow, is one of your clarinets. D'you know I've never been to an orchestral rehearsal before, but I'm staying with my sister for a while and Jeremy talked me into coming along. I must say I never dreamed that it was quite such a job to get everything together.'

Mr Roberts gives a wry smile. 'If you think this is hard work you should hear our junior orchestra; that's when you really do need patience, when they haven't actually got the technique to be able to play the notes securely. This lot are the best of the bunch; they'll put on a pretty decent performance when it comes to it.'

For a few minutes the two men chat quietly together, the one in search of information, the other imparting it. It seems that Mr Malcolm has come to music rather late in life.

'Never had much time for that sort of thing at school,' he says apologetically. 'Mad on games I was; just couldn't see the point of staying indoors scratching away on an out-of-tune fiddle. But I must say that lately I've been listening a lot, mostly on the car radio, and I really would like to get to know a bit more about it. I suppose I'm one of those maddening people who says 'I like what I know,' to which you'll probably reply 'How did you get to know it in the first place?'

'Exactly'. Mr Roberts gets to his feet a little less wearily. 'Tell you what; I'm on my way over to the music school now; why don't you come along and have a listen to what's going on up there?'

Involuntarily Mr Malcolm glances at his watch. 'I don't think I can now; I've got to take young Jeremy home. But could I come another day perhaps?'

'By all means. How are you fixed on Wednesday evening? I've got some really good young teachers on the staff now, fresh out of college, and Wednesday nights they get together and rehearse chamber music. Some of our better youngsters join in and then at the end of term we do a slap-up concert.'

To Mr Malcolm's ears the words 'chamber music' have a forbidding ring but he feels it would be impolite to refuse now, especially as he has expressed a wish to explore further.

'What sort of time?' he asks.

'Oh – sevenish; when you like really . . .'

On which somewhat vague note Mr Roberts makes for the exit, leaving his new-found acolyte to take Jeremy back to his parents.

The following Wednesday Mr Malcolm drives into the school grounds and parks his car in a small but deserted tarmac plot marked VISITORS in large white letters. Uncertain of his whereabouts in the autumnal darkness, he stands for a moment or two, listening. Distant strains of music drift into the night from a low compact building some way apart from the main block. With the cautiously restricted steps of someone treading unfamiliar ground and half expecting to tumble headlong over some unseen obstacle, he follows the sounds to their source. Entering the music school, he finds himself in a brightly-lit foyer liberally plastered with posters advertising concerts in the area; ahead of him a door marked Director of Music catches his eye. Wondering if a normally polite knock will register against the medley of instrumental sounds reverberating along the corridors, he raps the door-panel rather more firmly than he had intended. No invitation to come in is forthcoming; he is about to knock again when the door is opened abruptly. Mr Roberts extends a welcoming hand.

'So you've actually come', he says, smiling. 'Let's take a stroll along the corridor and pay a few calls; I've warned my colleagues that they might be having a visitor.'

As they approach a door marked Practice Room A, the sounds from within come into sharper focus, even though they remain elusive to Mr Malcolm's untutored ear. 'It's the Mozart clarinet quintet', says Mr Roberts in confidential tones. He opens the double-doors, and as the two men enter the sparsely furnished room, the players break off in mid-phrase. Introductions having been effected, the Director suggests they begin the movement again, 'from the top' as musicians say. Mr Malcolm squeezes into a corner, wondering if it would be foolish to ask why, if the work is called a clarinet quintet, there is only one clarinettist and a string quartet; surely it would be logical for a clarinet quintet to have five clarinets. . . . He quickly banishes the thought as Mozart's mellifluous opening phrase casts its spell, its gentle contour a soothing contrast to the clarinet's more athletic response.

If a work is called simply 'Quintet', 'Quartet' or 'Trio', it will almost certainly be for strings only; the contrasting instrument (if any) will be used as an aid to identification. Thus a clarinet quintet will indeed be for clarinet and string quartet, an oboe quartet will be for oboe and string *trio*, a piano trio for piano and *two* string instruments – violin and cello. There are a number of examples of slightly unusual combinations such as the so-called Horn Trio by Brahms which is for horn, violin and piano, or, to move to a larger scale, the Schubert Octet which is scored for clarinet, horn, bassoon, two violins, viola, cello and double bass. This perhaps sounds more like a miniature orchestra than a true chamber work, as opposed to the Mendelssohn Octet which is really for two string quartets – four violins, two violas and two cellos. The term 'chamber' music, with its regrettable tendency to cause embarrassed giggles amongst the young, is simply a literal translation of the German word for 'room', *Kammer*. It therefore implies music that is suitable in scale to be performed in the relative intimacy of a large drawing-room rather than a public concert-hall.

The actual combination of instruments is entirely at the composer's discretion; one could indeed have a quintet for five clarinets if one chose, although it would be prudent in such a case to use several different members of the clarinet family, such as the small and rather shrill 'E flat' clarinet at the top and the mellow bass clarinet at the lower end. Even so one would not call it a 'clarinet quintet' but a 'quintet for five clarinets'.

To the connoisseur, chamber music represents the highest form of musical art, partly because of the challenge imposed by the limitation of numbers, but mainly owing to the subtle interchange of ideas between the participants who must think and feel as one. Admittedly in the earlier string quartets of Haydn there is a tendency for the first violinist to hog the limelight, but this was soon to change, and all the great string quartets show a remarkable equality of interest between the four players. As the technical skills of string players developed, so the demands composers made on them became more challenging. One can hear this process very clearly in the great succession of quartets written by Beethoven. The set of six comprising Op. 18 were composed between 1798 and 1800; despite their remarkable individuality one can still trace their descent from Haydn. Between 1805 and 1806 he again turned his attention to quartet writing and produced the three 'Razumovsky' quartets Op. 59, so called after the Russian Count to whom they were dedicated. They show an enormous advance over the earlier set, being more expansive, more dramatic and more loosely constructed. Two more quartets followed in

1809 and 1810. A gap of thirteen years then ensued before Beethoven ventured into the medium again, thirteen years in which his concept of musical form changed radically. The last great quartets, judged by some to be the supreme achievement of his life, date from 1823 to 1826, Opp. 127, 130, 131, 132, 133 and 135. (Op. 133 is not a complete quartet but one gigantic movement lifted whole from Op. 130 and known as the *Grosse Fuge*, the Great Fugue.) These final quartets take us into an entirely different world of musical experience from anything written before, not only for their technical demands but also for the intricacy of the musical thought enshrined in them.

Roughly a century later the Hungarian composer Béla Bartók was to produce a nearly comparable monument to his genius with his six string quartets. As with Beethoven, they reveal a remarkable development of individuality, spread, in Bartók's case, over a period of thirty years. Their use of asymmetric rhythms, ferocious dissonance and angular melodies earned them few friends when they first appeared, but they are now acknowledged as masterpieces, and even an uninitiated audience will be moved to cheer, responding to the sheer physical excitement generated by the players as they meet the immense challenge of the music.

Works for keyboard and strings, 'Piano Quintets', 'Quartets' or 'Trios', present serious aesthetic problems. It is all too easy for the modern piano to dominate the scene, causing the strings to sound relatively ineffectual in a way that they would not if left to themselves. For example, the Schumann Piano Quintet, despite its amazing wealth of melodies, is unpopular with the string players since they feel that for much of the time they are reduced to a supportive role. Moreover, the actual means of tone production are so different that the sensitive ear finds it difficult to reconcile the percussive character of the piano with the smooth and sensuous quality of string tone. This applies to sonatas for piano and a single string instrument; for instance, Brahms tends to write such massive piano parts that even a cello risks being swamped. (There is a delightful story of Brahms rehearsing his second cello sonata with a somewhat indifferent player. At one point the labouring cellist cried pathetically 'I can't hear myself!' Brahms in his gruffest mood was heard to mutter 'You're lucky'.)

Such problems, needless to say, do not arise in the Mozart clarinet quintet to which we should now return as an ideal example of

chamber music at its most elegant. It opens with a serene melody
scored in an almost hymn-like way for the four string players

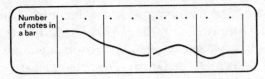

Fig. 24

(The curves represent the shape of the melody, the dots the number of notes
in each bar.)

A couple of bars later we find the first entry of the clarinet; the
passage could hardly be more different in character, a little fountain
of notes that rises through two octaves and then splashes down again.

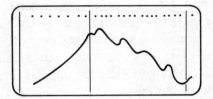

Fig. 25

Now these two ideas are so different in every respect that one might
feel that they could hardly be interchangeable; indeed Mozart
confirms this impression by repeating the dialogue, albeit somewhat
changed in detail. But no sooner has he done so than the two violinists
decide that they would like to try their hand at the 'fountain' theme,

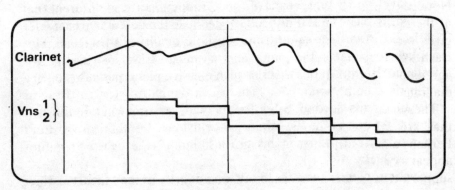

Fig. 26

and so they do, to delicious effect. The clarinet then introduces a new idea, at first smoothly gliding and then increasingly curvaceous. Beneath it, the two violins have a slow step-by-step descent, exactly synchronised as though hand in hand. (See Fig. 26)

A brief flutter of movement in the clarinet part brings a corresponding reaction from the violins, but then comes a wonderful exchange of roles. The cello imitates the clarinet's sinuous melody two octaves lower, so that what was previously the top line is shifted to the bass. Meanwhile the second violin and the viola start on the hand-in-hand descent, only to find that they get *out* of step, the viola dragging a pace behind.

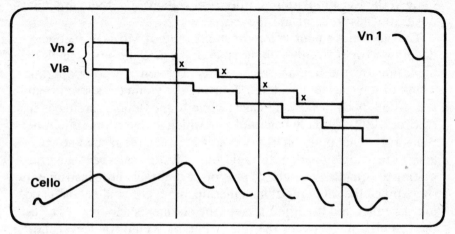

Fig. 27

Notice how the gap between the second violin and the viola narrows at the points marked with a cross, setting up a tension which then gives way as the viola makes its delayed step down. The resultant clashes give a delightful spice to the harmony, quite different from the agreement between the two descending parts in the preceding diagram.

The whole first movement is full of subtleties of this kind, passages that are apparently similar but wonderfully different in detail. Perhaps a little surprisingly, the Second Subject (remember Stella?) appears on the first violin, a gently curving melody in E major supported by sustained chords from the second violin and viola and a *pizzicato* (plucked) bass from the cello. Naturally we assume that the clarinet will copy the same pattern. Instead the strings, first violin included, set up an uneasy syncopated figure whose restlessness drives the clarinet into a quite unexpected *minor* key; in operatic terms this is a heroine distraught. Not surprisingly it leads to a considerable increase in emotional tension.

In the Development section we again find an intriguing exchange of roles. The clarinet is given the initial serene theme; the strings make considerable play with the 'fountain', each in turn making a cheerful splash while the clarinet remains a silent spectator. The central section becomes extremely active, with cascades of notes tumbling from violin, viola and cello in turn, while the clarinettist has a series of phrases which stride up and down as restlessly as a tiger in a cage. Only in the Recapitulation is order restored; even so there are many novel touches to captivate the ear.

The slow movement is a perfect example of Mozart's instinctive devotion to opera. Although the span of the melodic line exceeds the limitations of the human voice, the conception is wholly operatic. Think of the clarinet as a tenor courting the violin (as soprano) and the 'scene' becomes crystal clear. Initially the 'tenor' serenades his beloved with a limpidly beautiful aria which in due course elicits her reply. From that point on, the dialogue between them becomes more and more impassioned, with rapid but delicate scale-passages suggesting the quickening pulse of passion. Admittedly both instruments share much the same register, something no tenor could actually do, but the fuller and breathier tone of the clarinet is enough to suggest the essential maleness of the role, while the violin was never more essentially feminine than in this movement.

The Minuet that follows is rather more square in character, and here the lower strings are often given a chance to lead the melody while the first violin and the clarinet doodle away happily on a deliberately childish two-note theme. The plan of the movement is quite complex since it has two Trios, one without clarinet, one with. First the Minuet is played with repeats. (It is in two sections, one a mere eight bars, the other three times as long.) Then comes Trio 1, again in two sections – 16 bars then 24 – both of which are repeated. The Minuet is then played again *without* repeats, followed by Trio 2 whose two sections are respectively 12 and 38 bars long. These too are repeated, after which the Minuet is played one final time. It is as though Mozart was toying with the idea of combining the Minuet-Trio plan with the form of a Rondo since the irregular lengths of the two Trios give them something of the character of Episodes. Here is a plan of the movement:

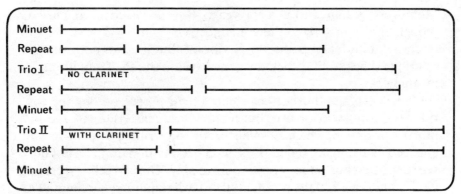

Fig. 28

To the casual listener the music sounds formal enough, but when the proportions are exposed as in this diagram, one realises how ingeniously Mozart exploited a combination of regularity and irregularity.

The finale is a set of variations on a theme that would be enjoyed equally in the nursery or in a grand ballroom. It is full of wit, exploiting the clarinet's agility to great effect in wide skips and nimble runs. The fifth variation is an *adagio* whose attempts to introduce a note of pathos need not be taken too seriously since its ultimate effect is to cause the theme to hasten to its conclusion, as though the players had suddenly become aware that the bar was about to close before they could get in their last orders.

Leaving the players to continue their rehearsal, Mr Roberts and Mr Malcolm discreetly withdraw.

'It's very graceful, isn't it', says Mr Malcolm, hoping that he's hit upon the right word to describe his reaction. 'It seems to take you right back to another age.'

'It's funny you should say that; I often say to my classes that music is like a time machine. Whenever you play a piece of music, providing you do it reasonably well, you rekindle the emotions of someone who could have been dead for centuries. For instance, have you ever heard any madrigals by Monteverdi?'

Mr Malcolm, only vaguely aware that Monteverdi was an Italian from a very long time back, admits that he hasn't.

'They're amazingly passionate. You know, one tends to think of early seventeenth-century music as something so remote that it belongs in a museum, and I can't say I'd get much kick out of seeing Monteverdi's nightshirt in a glass cage. But the *music* . . . It's just as though the man's right there in the room with you with all the intensity of his feelings absolutely vibrant. But it needs performance to bring it back to life; stick the copy back on the shelf and it's dead, meaningless.'

Mr Roberts's enthusiasm has halted their progress along the corridor for a moment or two, but he now leads his visitor to another practice-room in which a small group of string players are still engaged in arranging themselves in such a way that they can not only see each other but actually have room to play. The two cellists seem to be the main cause of the problem since each requires a fair amount of floor space. As the players mime the action of bowing to ensure that they have freedom to move, the leading violinist starts to tune, giving the customary A to her colleagues.

'What are they going to play?' whispers Mr Malcolm.

'Schubert,' comes the reply. 'The string quintet; some people reckon it's the finest work of its kind ever written. Notice the two cellos; some string quintets have two violas, Mozart's for instance, but perhaps that's because he liked to play the viola himself. Schubert wrote this in the last year of his life, 1828; he couldn't have left a more fitting monument.'

The sound of tuning dies away and the players seem to make a special mental effort to prepare themselves to play the opening chord, bows poised, expressions intent. Only the second cellist stays aloof; presumably his turn will come later. Pure and clear the first harmony emerges out of the expectant silence. It glows; then, with the increase of intensity, twists into a more impassioned dissonance only to return once more to the serenity of the opening. A fragment of a tune appears, the paired notes a little hesitant; violins and viola punctuate it with a high chord, soft and ethereal in effect. In sharp contrast Schubert now offers us a darkened version of the opening phrase, changing its character in two ways, partly by giving the top line to a cello instead of a violin, but even more by putting the music into a minor key. He then plays a subtle trick on us, giving the illusion that he has six instruments rather than five. A richly sombre three-note chord in the bass is answered by a more expressive (though still hushed) three-note chord two octaves higher. It is the viola which creates the illusion, supplying both the top note of the deep harmony and the bottom note of the more lofty reply. After these first, almost tentative beginnings, all five players soon find themselves at full stretch, the cellos combining forces in an impassioned melody in their darkest register while the three upper strings seem to strike sparks as though from an anvil. Suddenly the music appears to freeze on a single note sustained by the two cellos; we are at the brink of one of the most magical moments in all music. The second cello yields, drifting gently down from the sustained G to the E flat below. If Second Subjects tend by convention to be lyrical in character, this must be a supreme example, for now the two cellos embark on one of the most ravishingly beautiful tunes that even Schubert ever penned. The viola, never more versatile than in this work, provides a discreet bass, while the two violins supply gently fluttering harmonies that suggest the little gasps and sighs of a girl overwhelmed by her lover's ardent supplication. Once the tune has run its course, the whole process is repeated with the same sort of exchange of roles that Mozart exploits in his clarinet quintet. Now it is the violins' turn to sing the melody, the second cello provides the bass, the viola and the first cello supplying the essential harmonies. A long extension of the tune follows, led by the first violin, but with slightly more agitated accompanying figures adding a touch of urgency. To analyse the whole movement in these terms would become wearisome; 26 pages of score or 445 bars of music give evidence of the expansive scale that came naturally to Schubert. Yet despite its length it conforms remarkably closely to the basic precepts of sonata form, the conventional landmarks of First and Second Subjects, Bridge Passage, Development and Recapitulation all being clearly defined.

The slow movement that follows is one of Schubert's most perfect inspirations. The second violin, viola and first cello (the 'central' three players) sustain an immensely long melody that indeed tells of 'the peace that passeth all understanding'. The second cello gently plucks a minimal bass-line while, above, the first violin interpolates a number of indescribably touching little phrases, mere fragments that were obviously inspired by birdsong. (The very first of these corresponds exactly in rhythm to the voice of the quail in the slow movement of Beethoven's 'Pastoral' Symphony.) Although inspired by birdsong, this is no slavish copy of nightingale or lark. What is immediately apparent to even the most uninitiated listener is that this is night-music, a summer evening perhaps, but one in which the absolute stillness of the countryside casts an almost hypnotic spell.

The calm is dramatically shattered. An angry trill from all five players shifts the music into the alien key of F minor where, utterly unrelated to all that has gone before, Schubert introduces an impassioned melody on the first violin, reinforced an octave beneath by the first cello. As in Mozart the conception is operatic, a duet for soprano and tenor racked by the anguish of a forbidden love; but it is in a mood far removed from the tenderness of Mozart's clarinet quintet. The agitated syncopations of the accompanying harmonies and the violent menace implicit in the second cello part bring us remarkably close to Verdi opera at its most dramatic. At last this emotional storm burns itself out; as though bled dry, the music is reduced to silence, a silence broken only by suppressed tears. A quiet sustained chord, a veritable soothing hand, quells emotion; the opening tune returns. The three 'central' players resume their original serenity but the aftermath of the storm lingers on both in the second cello and the first violin parts. Although conducted in a whisper, their dialogue maintains a feeling of agitation that was wholly absent at the beginning of the movement; it is a long time before that initial calm is restored and we hear once again the snatches of birdsong. Three bars from the end of the movement, just as we feel confident that all strife is stilled, there is a sudden violent chord, a last stab of pain. It serves more than a purely emotional purpose, giving us a final reminder of F minor, the alien key of the central storm; but then 'Not again' says Schubert and with tender compassion returns to the restful haven of E major.

The Scherzo is robust and earthy, the two cellos providing a density to the harmony that shows that any imagined dancers are no longer in an aristocratic ballroom but in a barnyard. Yet, for all the heavy-booted character of the opening phrases, the movement is extremely fast and demands great agility as well as strength. A notable feature is the rapidity with which Schubert switches from one key to another so that, for instance, a tune that is totally committed to the key of E flat major will, without warning, be plunged into the quite contradictory tonality of B major. With a deft change of direction he will then switch back to C major, the 'home' key. Such surprise moves abound, but none is more surprising than the central Trio which provides a complete change of character. The rustic exuberance is replaced by melancholy sighs and darkly sonorous harmonies. Did Schubert have a vision of a spurned lover standing in the shadows, unable to bring himself to join in the general revelry? Such speculations are not too out of place since many of the songs he set with such prodigious facility deal with comparably romantic scenes. He himself was shy and self-effacing, while venereal disease made him feel cut off from any normally happy relationship with women. It is not entirely fanciful to suggest that this strangely introspective Trio may be something of a self-portrait.

The fourth movement, though abundantly endowed with captivating tunes, is not as remarkable as its predecessors in sheer originality. There are moments when the notes spin on without a sense of any great purpose, while at other times one feels that Schubert suddenly wishes to impress us with academic skills that his genius could easily dispense with. (Unbelievably he had actually applied to a noted teacher of the day, Simon Sechter, for lessons in counterpoint, but so far as we know his tragically early death prevented the plan from materialising.) The quintet was his last major instrumental work; less than two months after its completion he died, never having heard it performed in public although it is believed he may have heard a private rehearsal played by friends. It was not until 32 years later that the first public performance was given, a neglect of one of music's greatest masterpieces that seems quite inexplicable.

'I think we've got time for just one more visit,' said Mr Roberts softly as he and his visitor re-entered the corridor. 'Or have you had enough for one evening?'

'No, I'm fascinated. It's so different from just listening to a record or the radio. Seeing it all close up like this . . . well, I don't know, but it makes you realise how *physical* music is. I mean, you'd think those violins would crack under the strain. Those players really dig in, don't they.'

'Well, the actual style of string playing has changed enormously over the centuries. In the old days back in the time of people like Vivaldi and Bach they'd never have attacked the string like that; and they hadn't learnt the secret of how to cope with the highest register of the instrument either.'

'But those instruments are still in use aren't they? Surely if money's no object you buy a Strad don't you? I saw in the paper the other day "ITALIAN VIOLIN FETCHES RECORD PRICE" – and it was some amazing figure like £150,000 . . .'

'You don't surprise me; but whoever bought it wouldn't have got a genuine Strad.'

'What – you don't mean it was a fake?'

'Oh no; but when that violin left Signor Antonio Stradivari's workshop some time around 1700 its neck would have been shorter, the bridge would have been shallower, the finger-board – that's the black bit under the strings – would have been shorter, it wouldn't have had a chin-rest; in fact about the only original bits that are left on a Strad today are that cunningly shaped wooden box and the fancy bit at the far end called the scroll. And even the inside of the box has been strengthened and modified. It's still an amazing bit of carpentry though, or should I say joinery; d'you know that there are more than seventy pieces of wood in a violin and not a single screw to hold them together?'

Mr Malcolm, who's run up the odd set of bookshelves in his time, looks distinctly impressed.

'Well, that's one weight off my mind,' he says, chuckling; 'I don't think I'll bother buying one if it's that much of a botch-up . . .'

Together they reach the end door of the passage. Mr Roberts knocks and enters. The sole occupant is a violinist, her long dark hair swept back over her shoulder, her face slightly aquiline with deep-set eyes that reveal a trace of annoyance at being disturbed. On seeing who it is she smiles a mite more graciously, lowering the violin from her shoulder and placing the bow carefully on the nearby piano.

'Sara, this is Mr Malcolm; I'm in the process of converting him to music. What do you feel about running through the Franck for him – it'd be a good try-out for Saturday.'

'Well, I'm pretty tired, but if you really want to . . .'

'That's my girl.' Turning to his visitor, Mr Roberts continues, 'Sara and I are playing the César Franck violin sonata at a charity do on Saturday. She does it famously – played it for her performer's diploma when she left the Academy; but it's a helluva part for the pianist I can tell you. Franck must have had hands like a gorilla's; talk about *stretch* . . .'

Mr Malcolm is beginning to feel slightly at a loss, not even certain who this Franck person is – or was.

'I take it he's French,' he ventures a trifle hesitantly.

'Well, Belgian actually, but he spent most of his life in France. He was a fantastic organist but the French never really acknowledged his greatness as a composer until he was well into his sixties. He used to get up at 5.30 each morning, do a couple of hours' composition before breakfast, and then spend his days teaching for a pittance. Wouldn't suit me at all; I don't reckon my brain starts to turn over until about 11 o'clock in the morning. Sara, tell him about the first performance; its a marvellous story.'

Sara, who has been fastidiously polishing her violin with a soft yellow duster, looks up a little startled at the request.

'Oh, it was back in eighteen eighty-something ... um ...'86 I think. The sonata was dedicated to a famous violinist called Ysaÿe, and he and some woman pianist whose name I always forget were going to play it in an art gallery in Brussels.

The trouble was that because of the value of the pictures absolutely no artificial light was allowed. It was an afternoon concert of course but by the time they got to the Franck the light was beginning to fade. They coped with the first movement all right but by then they could hardly see the music. They were all for calling it off, but the audience urged them on until they gave in. Believe it or not they played the last three movements from memory, in the dark. It must have been really weird.'

'And when you see what I have to play in the last movements you'll realise what a fantastic feat that was,' adds Mr Roberts, sitting down at the piano and playing a few chords at random. He gives Sara the Statutory A and she spends a moment or two tuning punctiliously. Finally satisfied, she gives Mr Roberts a nod, then darts a quick glance at the stranger. 'Don't expect too much', she says disarmingly, 'I've been teaching all day.'

Accustomed as he has become to the idea that anything called a sonata is likely to start with a fairly positive gesture, Mr Malcolm is surprised at the quietness of the opening, four preliminary chords from the piano lead into a lyrical tune that sways gently to and fro in a beautifully relaxed manner. But gradually Sara's tone increases in intensity until the music builds to an impassioned climax. At once the pianist takes over as if welcoming the release from a subservient role. Although the music seems to lack rhythmic variety there's no denying its emotional impact ...

The César Franck sonata is a typical late romantic work possessing many features that make it notably different from anything written in the first half of the nineteenth century. The material is much more expansive than anything you would find in a violin sonata by Beethoven, the First Subject being a lyrical tune some 27 bars long. It is given wholly to the violin, the piano meanwhile supplying a cushion of rich harmonies with virtually nothing in the way of melodic interest or implied dialogue.

But no sooner has the violinist reached the climatic peak of her theme than the pianist takes over with a more openly passionate tune which we must assume to be the Second Subject despite the absence of any clearly identifiable Bridge Passage. For some time the pianist extends this theme on his own while the violin remains silent; indeed, one of the most intriguing structural features of the movement is the way in which the two instruments are allotted themes which they keep to themselves rather than sharing. At no point does the violinist attempt to steal the pianist's theme, even though it would sound splendid on the violin. Admittedly when the violin re-enters after the extensive piano solo there is a brief passage, a mere four bars, in which the two instruments do copy each other, but since the music is clearly transitional it can hardly be classified as a significant inter-change. The Development section, essentially the dramatic core of a classic sonata-form movement, is virtually non-existent, a contem-plative look at the basic shape of the initial theme over somewhat static harmonies. In a matter of seconds Franck embarks on his Recapitulation, exploiting the bell-like sonorities of the piano in a magical way that again would have been quite unheard of in Beeth-oven's time. Once more the violin part builds to its climax, once more the pianist has his little solo rhapsody; a tranquil coda brings the movement to an end.

Such is the nature of the music that although it can be seen to have the attributes of sonata form it could just as well be called '*Poème*'. The sharp contrasts of mood that we find in classical sonatas, the swift exchange of ideas between partners, the changes of character brought about during the Development, all these are absent. Instead we find music which is song-like and lyrical throughout, its content unashamedly emotional, its exploitation of sensuously beautiful harmony verging on self-indulgence. The nearest thing to a precedent is to be found in one of the late Beethoven piano sonatas, Op. 101 in A major. It too begins with a leisurely movement in a not dissimilar rhythm; it too tends to be 'all of a piece', lacking the abrupt contrasts we normally find in his work. Yet although in Beethoven's terms Op. 101 is an intensely romantic piece (though not in the daunting fugue with which it ends), placed beside the César Franck it will seem a model of restraint. Franck's harmonies are much more widely spaced, his themes more openly expressive, his exploitation of sonority a more calculated element.

The second movement may serve the function of a scherzo but it is far from being one in any traditional sense. The turbulent piano part suggests a storm at sea, with angry waves beating against a rocky shore only to fall back again in a cloud of spray. The violinist is given every opportunity to enjoy the rich sound of the lowest string (G), and it is worth mentioning that Franck originally conceived the work as a cello sonata, only transferring it to the violin at the insistent behest of Ysaÿe, to whom it was then dedicated.

Not surprisingly, since the music does not pretend to follow the conventional pattern of a scherzo, there is no Trio; but again we can find passages which serve a roughly similar function, a contrast of mood and tempo, a relaxation of the rhythmic impetus. However, the construction of the movement is very free, with occasional passages which are designed to sound like spontaneous improvisation. It is even possible to imprison it within the corset of sonata form if one is so inclined though the fit is distinctly uneasy at times.

The third movement is not only the most unorthodox but also the most interesting in structure. Franck draws our attention to this by calling it *Recitativo-Fantasia*. Normally associated with oratorio and opera, recitative is the term used for those short linking narratives accompanied by organ or harpsichord and leading into an aria or chorus of greater musical significance; in other words a musical 'reciting' of the narrative by a soloist in which enunciation of the words is of greater importance than melodic interest. The meaning of Fantasia is self-evident, implying as it does the idea of Fantasy, freedom for uninhibited flights of imagination. The conjunction of the two words as used by Franck is intriguing since recitatives are a somewhat formal convention whereas fantasias are implicity *in*formal and *un*conventional. In the event, what Franck produces might almost be described as a *cadenza*, the term used to define that part of a concerto in which the orchestra leaves the soloist to his own devices, partly to display his technical virtuosity but also to add his own thoughts about the material provided by the composer. Originally such cadenzas were supposedly improvised on the spot, although I suspect that most performers had worked something out beforehand. It seems, though, that composers became increasingly sceptical about the suitability of some performers' 'spontaneous' contributions, and from Beethoven's time onwards cadenzas were habitually written out as an integral part of the composition.

My reasons for classifying the third movement of the Franck sonata as a cadenza are three-fold. In the first place it is clearly meant to sound like an improvisation; it recalls and dwells on the main theme of the first movement; third, it prepares the way for one of the most important episodes in the fourth movement.

Like the first movement it begins with a four-bar introduction for the piano; that said, the mood could hardly be more different – the one soothing and serene, the other anguished and intense. Without going into the technicalities of harmony, the means by which these considerable differences of mood are achieved can be explained in reasonably comprehensible terms. The most obvious, but therefore most superficial, distinction is that the first movement begins with quiet chords which alternate at a very measured pace, one to each bar. In the third movement the chords begin strongly with three harmonies to a bar. It is the content of these chords which dictates the emotion; in the first movement the notes are agreeably consonant with each other across the whole span of four bars; in the third movement first the inner parts and then the top line move by a semitone, setting up grinding tensions in the harmony; each bar contradicts its predecessor. Close (chromatic) intervals such as Franck uses here are nearly always indicative of deep feeling whether they appear in an Elizabethan madrigal or Wagner's *Tristan and Isolde*.

The piano's lament is interrupted by the violin which, unaccompanied, launches into a free improvisation around the notes that comprise the tonality of E flat major. But by a subtle turn of phrase the music diverts into G minor, finishing quietly on the notes G→B♭ B♭ →G. Recognising something faintly familiar about this the pianist takes it up and with a conjuror's skill produces the main theme of the first movement, somewhat smoothed out, it is true, but clearly identifiable. The violinist echoes the last three notes, as if to underline their derivation. Again the pianist muses on the phrase, again he reminds us of the first movement. A deeply expressive phrase ensues, so clearly grief-stricken that one is entitled to interpret it as a lament for past joys. Is the sunny contentment of the first movement no longer attainable? It seems so, for a repeat of the violin cadenza no longer leads us back to such tender memories. Instead the music gradually gains impetus until a massive climax is reached. It quickly burns itself out as Franck leads us to the mysterious heart of the movement. Against a gently rippling accompaniment the violin spells out a slow tune of the utmost simplicity. At this stage we can have no idea that it is a premonition of a theme from the last movement, not even when it assumes a more dramatic manner, striding out boldly over an increasingly impassioned piano part. A little later on the violin too has tender recollections of the first movement but then resolutely rejects them. Yet, for all the forcefulness of this rejection the movement ends disconsolately, the quiet F sharp minor cadence giving no promise of the sunlight that is about to shed its radiance on us.

The last movement provides one of the most perfect examples of an intellectual device being used so effortlessly that it gives sheer joy to the listener. The *Canon* is what might be termed an adult version of a children's round. All of us who have sung 'Three Blind Mice' or 'Frère Jacques' are aware that everyone involved sings the same tune but starts at different times; the tune thus fits against itself in as many as four different places at once if it is a 'four-part' round. In its simple nursery forms the trick is not all that hard to manage since it is easy to devise a framework of straightforward harmonies upon which each segment of the tune can comfortably lie. In fact the two examples I have mentioned employ exactly similar techniques, and a little thought reveals that 'Three Blind Mice' is virtually an upside-down version of 'Frère Jacques', both rounds beginning with simple step-by-step progressions and ending with a more swiftly moving tail:

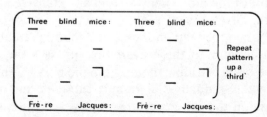

Fig. 29

The canon with which Franck so ingeniously begins the final movement of his violin sonata is a much more complex affair. The piano leads off with this shape:

Fig. 30

which is instantly copied by the violin an octave higher, the piano meanwhile continuing the melody into the next phrase:

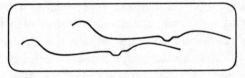

Fig. 31

and so they continue, the violin providing an exact shadow to the pianist's theme for some 37 bars. From a gentle beginning it drives on to a triumphant conclusion.

Against a smoothly flowing figure on the violin the piano now refers to the simple theme which the violin had hinted at in the mysterious central section of the previous movement (see p. 99). Soon it is the violinist's turn to lead off the canon with the pianist dutifully following. Once again, as is so often the case in chamber music, roles are exchanged, the violin being allotted the 'simple' tune, the piano having the smoothly flowing accompaniment. A new variant of the canon soon appears after two disarming false starts. (They are in the minor and Franck seems to be in no mood for melancholy.) This time the lead comes from the pianist's left hand which proves to be just as easy to follow.

In the centre of the movement we find an extensive and unexpectedly dramatic development section in which one segment of the canon theme is chopped out and subjected to rough treatment by the pianist. As a counter to these aggressive phrases the violinist re-introduces the boldly striding theme from the previous movement to dramatic effect. Gradually the tumult subsides and in the most endearing fashion the canon returns for the last time, bringing the movement to a glorious conclusion.

It may seem a trifle perverse to have introduced so unorthodox a sonata to illustrate this particular aspect of chamber music, but that is rather the point. The further one progresses through the nineteenth century the less likely one is to find any sonata that can be called 'orthodox'. The enduring strength of the form was its adaptability. More rigid forms such as the Fugue tended to become almost extinct except within the somewhat conservative confines of organ music, but the sonata-form concept survived, whether as symphony, concerto, chamber music or solo sonata. A violin sonata by Mozart speaks to us in a totally different language from that used by Franck. Mozart's piano, as we shall learn, was puny compared to an instrument of the 1880s, while even his violin would have been swamped by the later pianos. Yet despite the huge differences of idiom, the basic structure of such works can be seen to have much in common. It is for us to appreciate the line of inheritance that leads from one generation of composers to the next and to be aware not only of the obvious changes of style but of the less striking but nevertheless progressive chain of continuity.

10 _A pride of pianos_____

Over the following few weeks Mr Malcolm became quite a regular
visitor to the school. Childless himself, he was refreshed by the
cheerful enthusiasm of the young and it wasn't long before he knew
quite a few of the orchestra by name. During the coffee break he
would stand in the queue with them, chatting about whatever work
they had been rehearsing. He would help Miss Stebbing gather up the
substantial piles of music at the end of the morning, or lend a hand as
the bulky percussion instruments were stowed away in the store-
room behind the stage. He even attended the charity concert at which
Sara and Mr Roberts played the César Franck sonata; the splendid
panache displayed by the pianist more than compensated for the
occasional glaring inaccuracies. His initial acquaintance with the
music master ripened into friendship and he was delighted when one
day Mr Roberts invited him to 'drop in for a bite to eat one evening,
and have a look at my pianos'. Somehow he had never imagined that
anyone would have more than one piano in a house and he wondered
how many there would be and where they might be kept.

It was during the Christmas holiday that he first made his way to
John Roberts's home, a rather shabby old Victorian house set on a
slope well above street-level. The garden looked distinctly unkempt
and was clearly of little importance to the owner. A tug on the
old-fashioned bell-pull seemed to produce no response so he tried the
heavy cast-iron knocker. He was about to knock again when he heard
footsteps beyond the door. With a beaming smile John welcomed him
in.

'You found it all right, then?'

'Oh yes, no problem. I tried the bell . . .'

'Sorry, I should have warned you. I never have got round to fixing
it; in fact I'm not sure how to. Anyway, come in and get warm; let me
take your coat . . .'

The house, though spacious, had clearly seen better days. Presumably built for some prosperous Victorian merchant, the rooms were

lofty with some quite ornate plaster-work decorating the ceilings. A rather pretentious mantlepiece framed a fine open fireplace whose cheerful blaze made a welcome sight on such a wintry night. Books and scores were crammed into shelves in disorderly fashion while an elaborate music-centre provided a curiously incongruous touch of space-age modernity in contrast to the rather dilapidated furniture. Holding the proffered glass of sherry, Mr Malcolm, neat and orderly soul that he was, surveyed the scene with slight dismay. It was only then that he noticed the pianos, three of them, at the farther end of the room, as yet still in half-darkness. Seeing the direction of his gaze, John flicked a couple of switches by the door and flooded the room with light.

'There you are', he said. 'My beloved Steinway which belonged to my mother. That one over there's a Broadwood dated 1846, and then there's the square piano which I reckon must be around 1810.'

Mr Malcolm had never even heard of a square piano and approached it with some interest. 'You don't mean to tell me that Beethoven used to play on something like *this*', he said with a slight note of incredulity.

'Oh yes; mind you, the square piano and something much nearer in shape to our grand pianos both existed at the same time. Haydn had a very grand 'grand' piano towards the end of his life, yet his piano music isn't nearly as demanding as Beethoven's.'

'How did the two shapes evolve? They look like quite different instruments apart from the keyboards.'

'Well, curiously enough the grand came first. It got its shape from the harpsichord, but you mustn't confuse the two; they work on totally different principles. The strings on a harpsichord are plucked by a quill, a sort of cross between a piano and a guitar. With the piano the strings are struck by little hammers. Originally the hammers were covered with leather so the tone lacks the sort of bloom we get today with soft felt covers. You can hear there's a tremendous difference.'

John sat down at the square piano and began to play the opening bars of the 'Moonlight' Sonata. To Mr Malcolm it sounded a bit twangy, while the bass notes seemed to lack sustaining power. He could see that the strings stretched from left to right at a slight angle so that they were not quite parallel to the keyboard. After a moment or two John got up and went over to the Steinway grand. He began to play the same music. The difference was remarkable, the sound so much richer, the bass marvellously sustained, the melody more clearly defined. Even the pitch was different, the Steinway sounding substantially higher.

'Are you playing it in a different key?' asked Mr Malcolm.

'Not exactly', said John. 'But during the nineteenth century there was a general desire for more brilliance and the accepted pitch rose so much that square pianos like that just couldn't take the strain of the increased tension in the strings. If I tuned that one up to modern concert pitch I'd be in all sorts of troubles – broken strings and probably a twisted frame. Anyway, it'd never stay in tune. It raises an interesting point though, because when we hear sopranos complaining that the finale of Beethoven's Choral Symphony is much too high, they forget that Beethoven didn't expect them to sing way up there; he would have imagined the music at least a semitone lower.'

'Why did they make these square pianos, then, when that sort of triangular shape seems so much more satisfactory?'

'Well, the square shape derives from another early instrument, the clavichord, which co-existed with the harpsichord. I've got one in the next room; I'll show it to you if you like.'

The two men crossed the passage into an altogether cosier room where an instrument the size of a small writing table stood against the wall. John opened the lid, revealing the same left-to-right arrangement of the 'strings' which, being made of fine brass wire, gleamed golden in the light. The inside of the lid was decorated with an elegant design whose original colouring had faded somewhat over the centuries. The keyboard seemed distinctly unusual, with the positions of the black and white notes reversed; the keys seemed narrower too, as though made with a woman's hand in mind.

'If you live in a modern block of flats this is the perfect instrument,' said John, smiling. 'You could play it all night and the neighbours would never hear you. Listen . . .'

He started to play, his fingers clinging closely to the keys. The sound was unbelievably delicate, almost fairy-like, and it seemed that the notes could actually be made to vary slightly in pitch, imparting a strange melancholy to the tune.

'You see how simple the action is – it's just like a see-saw really. Each note is like a lever; I press down one end and the other end rises by a corresponding amount. That little brass tooth there makes direct contact with the string; in fact if I press too hard you can see the string actually stretch.'

John increased the pressure on the key and the tiny sound seemed almost to wail in protest.

'It's the only keyboard instrument you can actually vibrato on, only instead of vibrating my finger tip from side to side as a string-player does, I have to make a minute up-and-down motion. Definitely not an instrument for the heavy-handed. . . . Anyway, you can see how similar in shape it is to the square piano, though the action of the piano is much more complicated. To get a bigger sound the hammer must be thrown at the string, a bit like a miniature catapult. What you lose of course is this intimate contact with the string that gives the clavichord its unique quality.'

With obvious delight he began to play 'Greensleeves', lingering expressively on certain notes to demonstrate the delicate vibrato.

'And this would date from . . . ?' asked Mr Malcolm once the piece was ended.

'Oh, the clavichord's been around since the fifteenth century at least but the earliest surviving one is dated 1543. It's in a museum in Leipzig. This one was originally made in 1660 but it was in a right old mess when I bought it. It took a friend of mine the best part of a year to restore it. Anyway, what about a bite to eat? Mary's staying with her mother for a few days so I'm afraid it'll be distinctly pot-luck; cooking is definitely not my forte.'

Suffering slightly from the after-effects of Christmas, Mr Malcolm was quite happy to have a somewhat frugal meal. Afterwards they returned to the big room; to his great delight he found that John needed little persuasion to settle down at the Steinway and start to play.

The entire development of changing styles in keyboard music is intimately bound up with the way in which the instruments themselves changed over the years. Although we often hear Bach's music played on the piano, it should be realised that Bach never wrote a note of piano music in his life. He reputedly tried a 'fortepiano' (as it was then known) at the court of King Frederick the Great in Potsdam in 1747, but was not greatly impressed. However his eldest son, Carl Philipp Emanuel, had every incentive to develop a genuine feeling for the piano since, as court composer at Potsdam, he had access to no less than fifteen of them. Even so he appears to have preferred the clavichord as still the more expressive instrument. The word 'fortepiano', literally 'loud-soft', was chosen to emphasise the instrument's one great advantage over the harpsichord, the ability to produce variations in volume by touch alone. The grandest harp-sichords could indeed provide a wide variety of tone-colours but they were produced in a rather complicated and essentially mechanical way.

To demonstrate the point, suppose that one plays the single note 'middle' C on a harpsichord. To produce any sound at all one of several 'stops', or in some cases 'pedals', must be engaged. (In this respect the harpsichord is similar to an organ, but there the resem-blance ends.) The 8-foot stop will produce the same middle C that we would expect to hear from a piano, but with the 16-foot stop engaged, the sound produced *from the same key* will be an octave lower. Engage the 4-foot stop and the same key will produce the C an octave higher. Thus a single key is capable of producing three different sounds. With the aid of a further mechanical device known as a 'coupler' it is possible to combine these so that the same key can sound two or three C's at different pitches simultaneously. Further variety can be produced with the addition of a second keyboard, or manual, which usually contained a 'lute' stop for soft effects. The sheer ingenuity that went into the design of such an instrument is something to marvel at, and it is only proper that the harpsichord has enjoyed such a revival in popularity in recent times.

There was indeed a period when harpsichord and fortepiano co-existed, rather as the horse and carriage and the motor-car did at the start of our own century. But the fortepiano, originally a some-what feeble-toned instrument, was constantly being improved by the makers and in time almost totally displaced its handsome predeces-sor. If Bach never wrote a piano piece, it is equally true to say that Beethoven never wrote a harpsichord piece, unless perhaps when he was still a boy.

For the ordinary music lover, the age of true piano music began with the era of Haydn and Mozart. (The reason for converting the word 'fortepiano' to the now universally accepted 'pianoforte' seems to be something of a mystery.) Keyboard players who had been brought up on the harpsichord had to learn an entirely new approach, cultivating subtle variations of tone that had hitherto been impossible to achieve. This explains the somewhat eccentric-looking use of the symbols *f* and *p* (*forte* and *piano*) that sometimes occurs in the music of this period. For instance Mozart may have a short sequence of notes, to be played not all that slowly, each one of which is marked in contradictory fashion:

p f p f p

The present-day student, accustomed to a wide range of volume, will tend to exaggerate this, producing a jerky effect where all that Mozart required was an emotional stress.

Both Haydn and Mozart wrote prodigious quantities of piano music, but it was Mozart, not only more widely travelled but also far more in demand as a concert performer, who perfected the piano concerto as a musical form. The idea of combining a virtuoso soloist with an orchestra was nothing new, as innumerable concertos for string and wind instruments from the seventeenth and eighteenth centuries indicate. Harpsichord concertos were not as abundant since the instrument was easily swamped by an orchestra of any size. However, by the time Mozart had reached manhood, the combination of piano and orchestra had become a more practical proposition. The problem of balance remained but could largely be solved by suppressing the orchestra whenever the soloist had any passage of importance.

I have already suggested that concertos are very similar in form to symphonies except for the addition of a solo protagonist. The first movement is normally in sonata form and in this respect the convention of repeating the Exposition proved to be valuable since the initial presentation of the material could be made by the orchestra, while the equivalent to the repeat could then be modified and elaborated by soloist and orchestra combined. With characteristic genius Mozart not only saw a potential hazard here but devised a brilliant way round it. In his large-scale concertos, which employ wind and brass as well as the customary strings, it was only too easy for the solo piano's tone to seem weak by comparison after a long and possibly dramatic orchestral exposition. (The '*tutti*' to use the proper term.) For the soloist to present, unsupported, themes that had already been heard on the full orchestra would inevitably seem to diminish his stature. It was for this reason that Mozart hit upon the idea of introducing the soloist with a new theme of a relatively slight character which would remain his and his alone. Thus in the great concerto in C minor (known as K.491 after the catalogue of his works made by Köchel) the soloist never actually plays the stern unison subject with which the work begins.

Instead the piano enters on a note of pathos, instantly establishing individuality but also making it clear that there is going to be no trial of strength.

Not until the Fifth Concerto of Beethoven, the 'Emperor' (1809), does the piano really stand up to the orchestra in the dominating manner which thereafter became the fashion. It was a gesture of defiance only made possible by the provision of a more powerful instrument whose greater sonority gave the soloist a chance of victory in what, up to then, had been an unequal contest.

Just as the Beethoven quartets reveal ever greater challenges to the technical skills of the performers, so do the piano sonatas. The most ferociously difficult is the so-called '*Hammerklavier*' Op. 106 (1818) which stretches the resources of the piano as far as they would go. (Its title has a slightly misleading significance to the English ear since it is simply the German word for piano.) The Golden Age of keyboard music really dawned just after Beethoven's death with the advent of composers such as Schumann, Chopin, Liszt and Brahms. Again, their style was influenced by the continual improvements that the piano manufacturers were introducing to meet an overwhelming popular demand.

While Mozart's piano was limited to a compass of five octaves, the keyboard of Chopin's time was extended to seven; the more potent sustaining pedal enabled new effects of mingled sonorities to be achieved; the range of tone was greatly amplified. The pianistic lions of the day were fêted with an hysteria not far removed from that accorded to the pop stars of today, and although much of the music performed was shallow and meretricious, the truly gifted composers found the piano an ideal medium for the expression of the most impassioned and romantic sentiments.

With the new pianistic resources made available to them, composers were quick to devise new techniques; the emphasis on dexterity of fingers which is so noticeable in the running passages one finds in Mozart or early Beethoven gave way to a method which employed arm, wrist and hand as one supple swiftly moving unit. The whole texture of music tended to become richer, an effect partly achieved by opening out supporting harmonies so that the hand extended beyond the confines of an octave. Mozart's accompanying figures seldom stretch the hand from a normally relaxed position; Chopin at times demands what appear to be superhuman stretches that can be managed only with the aid of a huge lateral movement of the wrist. Place the central finger of your left hand some six or seven inches above your knee, resting on top of the thigh. Now touch alternately your knee with your little finger and your hip-bone with your thumb, using the central finger as a pivot which never loses contact. Do this fairly rapidly and it will give you some idea of the flexibility and athleticism Chopin demands of his performers, and this in only one respect.

Chopin, Liszt, Schumann and Brahms all wrote numbers of studies designed to exploit and develop virtuosity. But preoccupation with technique was not the be-all and end-all, and a great deal of nineteenth-century romantic piano music is concerned with a quite open display of emotion that composers of Mozart's era would have found too explicit. The poetic beauty of the Chopin Nocturnes, the quiet heart-searching of the more intimate pieces of Brahms, the dreamy musings of Schumann are just as essential an aspect of the Romantic movement as the heroic rhetoric of Liszt or Tchaikovsky.

By the turn of the century there were signs that the full tide of romanticism was on the wane. Two notable new schools developed, one in France, the other in Russia.

It was the French composer Debussy (1862–1918) who perhaps made the most individual contribution. By using harmonies based on a six-note scale that omitted the intervals of a semitone

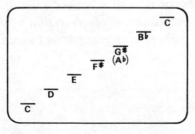

Fig. 32

(Cf. the scales shown in Figs. 18–20.)

he was able to create a marvellously atmospheric sound, vague and nebulous in comparison to conventional harmony, but entirely suited to his imaginative and pictorial conceptions. In all fairness, credit for the invention of this scale-formation must go to Liszt, who used it in some remarkably prophetic pieces that he wrote in the closing years of his life. Unfortunately it proved to have limitations as a new basis for composition and Debussy explored its potential to the full. Anyone using it thereafter would instantly be accused of copying him. Debussy's great fellow-countryman Ravel (1875–1937) managed for the most part to avoid the accusation; his piano music, brilliantly conceived for the keyboard despite his own limited abilities as a pianist, could be described as a French extension of Liszt's style, though generalisations of the sort are dangerous.

The second school, emanating from Russia, took a very different line. Admittedly Rakhmaninov was doing his utmost to continue a self-indulgent style of Romanticism, but we tend to forget that his ever-popular Second Concerto was written as early as 1901. It was the young Prokofiev (1891–1953) who was to introduce in his piano writing a steely percussive brilliance that blew away the last vestiges of Romantic sentiment. His savage attack on the traditional concept of how best to write for the piano was reinforced by the Hungarian Béla Bartók (1881–1945) whose piano music was also intensely anti-Romantic in character, exploiting dissonance in a way that excited virulent criticism. The Golden Days of pianism were disappearing in a violently fiery sunset, so much so that in recent years the piano itself has been subjected to the indignities of electronic distortion; its strings have even been 'prepared' for specific works by the insertion of foreign objects ranging from nuts and bolts to milk bottles. Perhaps most sadly of all, the relationship between the amateur pianist and the composer has been rudely severed so that anyone who plays for pure pleasure is unlikely to tackle anything of significance written in the last fifty years.

11 — Choral favourite

'No, not USSA!' yelled Mr Roberts. 'You make it sound as though he's a Viking raider – Ussa the Scourge of the North! It's "us a", "For unto *us a* child is born . . ." And it's still trudging along much too heavily; keep it light; you should be dancing with joy, not tramping round like a lot of policemen.' He turns to the pianist: 'just a couple of bars will do Tim, and tenors, I know there aren't many of you but don't try and make up for it by shouting. Right, off we go, and CONCENTRATE!'

Easter is not far away and several local choirs are combining with the orchestra in a selection of choruses from Handel's *Messiah*. The conductor had actually tried to persuade Mr Malcolm to join the choir, but his inability to read music had made him hold back even though it was the one choral work with which he could at least claim some familiarity. All the same, he had become positively addicted to rehearsals and was continually fascinated to observe the way in which performances grew stage by stage.

Handel composed his *Messiah* with exceptional fluency even by his standards; he noted that he began work on 22 August 1741. By 14 September the entire composition was completed in full score; one would imagine the effort to have left him exhausted, but within days he started to compose the oratorio *Samson*, the first part of which was finished a mere fortnight after he had penned the final Amen of the *Messiah*. Meanwhile copyists were put to work to prepare the music for choir, soloists and orchestra, a mammoth task which in these days of instant photocopying we tend to forget. Each individual chorus part had to be written out by hand; in such circumstances it was inevitable that errors would appear. On his way to Dublin in November of the same year, Handel, ever a practical musician, thought it might be prudent to get some singers to read through the hastily written parts so that time might be saved when rehearsals began in Dublin, where the first performance was to be given. Dr Charles Burney, the most noted of eighteenth-century musicologists, tells the story amusingly. It seems that Handel was stranded in Chester for several days owing to unfavourable winds in the notorious Irish Channel.

> During this time, he applied to Mr Baker, the Organist, to know whether there were any choirmen in the cathedral who could sing *at sight*; as he wished to prove some books that had been hastily transcribed, by trying the choruses which he intended to perform in Ireland. Mr Baker mentioned some of the most likely singers then in Chester, and among the rest a printer of the name of Janson, who had a good base voice, and was one of the best musicians in the choir . . . A time was fixed for this private rehearsal at the *Golden Falcon*, where Handel was quartered; but, alas! on trial of the chorus in the Messiah '*And with his stripes we are healed*', poor Janson, after repeated attempts, failed so egregiously, that Handel let loose his great bear upon him; and after swearing in four or five languages, cried out in broken English, 'You shcountrell! tit you not dell me dat you could sing at soite?' – 'Yes, sir,' says the printer, 'and so I can, but not at *first sight*.'

Six months after his arrival in Dublin, Handel directed the first performance of his *Messiah*. The work has such sacred associations for us that it comes as something of a surprise to learn that it was first given in the 'Musick Hall' in Fishamble Street. A particular request was made in the preliminary announcements that ladies should not wear hooped skirts nor gentlemen swords so as to make more space available for the large attendance expected. The work was received with rapture, as the *Dublin Gazette* reported:

> Words are wanting to express the exquisite delight it afforded to the admiring crowded Audience. The Sublime, the Grand, and the Tender, adapted to the most elevated, majestick and moving Words, conspired to transport and charm the ravished Heart and Ear.

After such a triumph, Handel must have been disappointed by the relative failure of the work when it subsequently received its first London performance at Covent Garden on 23rd March 1743, a

failure which seems inexplicable to us today. However, it should be
remembered that the form of the work was uncharacteristic. Handel
was essentially a man of the theatre and London society regarded him
primarily as an operatic composer. Of the many so-called oratorios
that he wrote only two, *Israel in Egypt* and *Messiah* were composed to
biblical words. Even Jennens, the reputed librettist of the *Messiah*
(though his private chaplain the Rev. Pooley selected much of the
text) described the work as 'an entertainment'. To the audience of the
day it must have seemed to be something of a hybrid; lacking a
continuing dramatic narrative it could hardly be considered as a
religious opera; but neither did it comply with any of the liturgical
forms used in acts of worship.

During the nineteenth century a somewhat misleading aura of
sanctity was superimposed on Handel's music so that he came to be
regarded as a religious rather than a theatrical composer. Those who
wish to perpetuate this dubious tradition should be reminded that
several of the best-loved choruses in his *Messiah* are transcriptions of
secular love-duets that he had composed for private concerts in
Londonderry House the preceding year. Never loath to recycle his
own (or indeed other people's) music, Handel doubtless thought that
they were unlikely to be performed again in their original form. Why
waste good tunes when they could usefully be served up again in a
new guise?

The *Sinfonia* or overture with which the work begins is in a style
developed by the great French composers Lully and Rameau, a slow
introduction of a rather severe nature followed by a swifter movement treated in a fugal manner. It is a purely instrumental movement
that would readily transplant into the theatre-pit, and reveals a very
different attitude from that shown by Bach in the massive opening
choruses of the St Matthew and St John Passions. Admittedly Bach
begins both works with a lengthy and impressive preamble for
orchestra, but these introductory pages lead directly to the chorus
and continue with similar figuration after the singers have made their
entry. Bach's introductions are integral; Handel's is detached. Indeed
the sheer vigour of the closing bars of the opening Sinfonia in no way
prepares us for the serene beauty of the music that immediately
follows, 'Comfort ye my people'. Handel describes this as a recitative
but it is an uncommonly lyrical one, accompanied not by the conventional keyboard instrument but by the strings playing in rich

harmony. Only in the final bars, 'The voice of him that crieth in the wilderness' does the music conform to the convention that the term recitative normally implies, the voice declamatory, the harmonies simply emphasising the main beats.

The ensuing aria 'Ev'ry valley', is in Handel's best operatic style and could as easily be allotted to Orpheus setting out to find Eurydice as to the prophet Isaiah in the desert. The extended treatment of the word 'exalted' is typical of the vividly descriptive way in which composers of the era married music to words. The extension of the second syllable alone through no less than forty-six notes is utterly unrealistic in terms of speech; but when one appreciates the *shape* of the phrase, which seems to leap buoyantly from one foothold to another while the accompanying chords underline the steepness of the ascent, one realises the total aptness of the setting. Not only does it describe the physical act of climbing out of the valley but also the spiritual exaltation that the climber feels within himself. Compare the vigour and agility of this phrase with the sustained smoothness of the word 'plain' and we realise that though Handel's English accent may have been atrocious, his comprehension of the deepest significance of words could not be faulted. More of a problem, as for all who try to speak a foreign language, was accentuation. Here he does blunder from time to time, as for instance with the word 'incorruptible' which he set as incorrup-*ti*-ble. He also follows the Italian practice, which he had certainly acquired during the few years he had spent there as a young man, of running the final vowel of one word into the initial vowel of its successor. 'Glo-*ryof* the Lord' has presented a problem to choir-trainers through many a rehearsal – hence the riddle 'Who is the Russian spy in Handel's Messiah?' to which the answer is 'Gloriov'.

Handel's writing for the chorus is masterly in its avoidance of cliché. If one comes to the work for the first time, it is impossible to predict the format of any chorus in advance. Admittedly, like most of his contemporaries, he shows a slight preference for beginning with one part only, though this may have been partly for the very practical reason that it is easier to set the correct tempo for a piece with a single line than with a massed choir. If we examine the structure of the first chorus, 'And the glory of the Lord', we can see how varied the textures are, how unpredictable the next event. After the cheerful introductory bars from the orchestra, he begins with altos alone; but their single line is answered by block harmony from soprano, tenor and bass, in which the altos, having regained their breath, also join.

Sop.		And the glory the glory of the	Lord
Alt.	And the glory the glory of the	Lord, the glory of the	Lord
Ten.		And the glory the glory of the	Lord
Bass.		And the glory the glory of the	Lord

Fig. 33

The tenors now take over the lead, and we might be forgiven for assuming that a more or less similar pattern may well be followed. It was an age in which symmetry and balance were highly regarded. Instead, we find a sequence of overlapping entries, the basses so eager to 'reveal the glory' that they cannot even wait for the tenors to finish their phrase.

Sop.		Shall be re——veal———ed	
Ten.	Shall be re—veal——ed		And the glory of the
Bass		Shall be re —veal—ed	shall be—re —

Sop.		And the glory the glory of the Lord —	shall
Alt.		shall be re—veal'd, shall be re——veal	————————
Ten.	Lord——		shall be re—veal——ed
Bass	—vealėd		

Sop.	be re—	veal'd.	And the glory, the glory of the Lord shall be revealed
Alt.	————	ed.	And the glory, the glory of the Lord shall be revealed
Ten.			And the glory, the glory of the Lord shall be revealed
Bass			And the glory, the glory of the Lord shall be revealed

Fig. 34

One thing Handel 'reveals' here is that the opening phrase 'And the glory . . .' fits in perfect counterpoint against its sequel, 'Shall be revealed'. The disclosure is made first by the tenors and basses and then endorsed by the sopranos and altos. But notice too after so many short phrases at almost the pace of natural speech, how effective and surprising is the long (four-bar) extension of the middle syllable -*veal*- in the alto part, a line which seems to draw the other parts in to the joyful combined affirmation of the message that ensues.

A brief orchestral interlude leads to a completely new idea, suggested I am convinced by the chiming of bells. The altos have it first – 'And all flesh shall see it together'. (The tenors reply and here again there is a surprise, the single unaccompanied line answered by another alike. One would expect at least two parts to overlap at this point.) Suddenly, and again the suggestion is of a great bell clanging, tenors and basses join in unison, 'For . . . the . . . mouth . . . of . . . the Lord hath spo-ken it', only dividing for the final two words. Above them sopranos and altos moving in parallel reiterate the earlier bell-like theme. The sopranos now, like a smaller treble bell, make as if to copy the resonant unison of the tenors and basses. Our natural expectation is that the pattern will be repeated, the sopranos perhaps being joined by the altos as reinforcements, the tenors and basses supplying the answering chime. Instead, Handel slightly compresses the soprano part (seven bars are reduced to six) while the three lower voices come in together *en bloc*.

How many thousands of times have choirs the world over rehearsed and performed this chorus without giving the least consideration to the constant inventiveness that Handel shows in juggling with such essentially simple material? We may sing the notes with suitably joyous enthusiasm but the ingenuity of the structure we take for granted.

In the course of his many operatic ventures it is hardly surprising that Handel came across some outstanding singers. (There were others with whom he quarrelled violently but they need not concern us here.) A much-admired favourite was the Italian male alto Gaetano Guadagni, and it was to demonstrate his talent that Handel re-wrote the aria 'But who may abide the day of his coming?' some nine years after he had first completed the score. In the original version, which was for bass voice, the sizzlingly exciting passages about 'the refiner's fire' simply do not exist. The new central section written for Guadagni's benefit is, as might be expected, a totally operatic conception. It could be classified as a typical 'revenge' aria, vowing death and destruction to a hated rival. Although it is one of the most magnificent sections in the entire oratorio, it always seems to me to sit uneasily in its context, and its blatantly operatic idiom highlights the difference between Handel and Bach in large-scale religious works. Bach is perfectly capable of writing music of savage intensity, but he will give it to the chorus, not to a soloist. His soloists contemplate the drama and share in the sufferings of Christ; but they are not allowed to draw attention to themselves as virtuoso singers, however technically difficult their parts may be to sing.

If one had to pinpoint the one passage in the *Messiah* that comes nearest in spirit to Bach it would surely have to be the wonderful bass recitative, 'For behold, darkness shall cover the earth'. The orchestral accompaniment, the notes paired off and heavily stressed, uses a type of figure that crops up many times in Bach. What Bach would not have allowed himself is the simple throbbing accompaniment unadorned by counterpoint that supports the glorious vocal line once the music modulates into the major. 'But the Lord shall arise upon thee, and his glory shall be seen upon thee.' The simplicity of the setting gives the music great majesty, and it is interesting to compare the treatment of the word 'rise' in this context to that of 'exalted' in 'Ev'ry valley'. In the opening tenor recitative I have already drawn attention to the eagerness with which the prophet climbs out of the valley; the music is young, exuberant. But when 'the Lord shall arise', although the idea of a decorated ascending phrase has a superficial similarity, the accompaniment gives tremendous dignity to the image.

The charming string interlude which we know as the 'Pastoral Symphony' – a rather different proposition from Beethoven's – was originally a mere eleven-bar introduction to the Shepherd's scene. Handel called it Pifa, from the Italian Pifarro, a primitive wind instrument played by peasants in the fields. Becoming enchanted with his own idea, he could not resist the temptation to extend it to its present length. It is very typical of what Purcell would have called a 'Curtain Tune', music to be played between scenes to get the audience into a suitable mood for coming events.

Handel's sense of theatre becomes very apparent with the complete change of pace that comes during the scene with the Angels and Shepherds; not that the music is so much faster in tempo but that the individual sections become so much more compact. Notice too the pulsating light when the Angel first descends, which becomes a dazzling glitter when the 'multitude of the heavenly host' appears, their wings iridescent and shimmering.

The second part of the oratorio, the Easter music, shows a notable change of style. Up to this point the music can fairly be said to have been – to adopt Jennens's own word – 'entertaining'. Now, for virtually the first time, it becomes truly profound, filled with a religious fervour that finally severs any putative link with the operatic stage. One cannot imagine the music of 'Behold the Lamb of God' being given to a chorus of captive slaves shortly to be released by some mythological hero. The opening phrase consists of a swift rising octave followed by a jerky descent on whose third note there is a shuddering trill. Surely the image in Handel's mind must have been of Christ heaving the cross on to his shoulder and literally staggering under its weight. The rhythm is such that one gets the impression of tremendous physical effort, and the choir should bring an almost painful intensity to their singing. Yet once we reach the phrase 'that taketh away the sin of the world' the music settles on to a single note beneath which the lower voice introduces a soothing gesture designed to dispel the agony of the initial pages.

The ensuing aria 'He was despised' also reveals a depth of feeling that is unmatched by anything in Part I. Whereas in 'The people that walked in darkness' the singer describes something that he is not experiencing himself, the alto soloist here *shares* the suffering of the Man of Sorrows. The brief three-note phrases that interrupt the vocal line are a touching symbol of tears. As in the solo arias in the Bach Passions, the singer so identifies with Christ that she wants to take his pain upon herself. (At the first performance it was sung so affectingly by Mrs Cibber that a member of the audience cried out 'Woman, for this thy sins be forgiven thee.') The central section, 'He gave his back to the smiters', shows Handel using an identical rhythm to that chosen by Bach to symbolise the relentless lash of the whip, though both composers distance the scene by marking the string parts 'soft'. A comparable rhythm spills over into the ensuing chorus as though the image of the lacerated back cannot be banished from our minds. 'Surely he hath borne our griefs and carried our sorrows' is the first chorus in the entire work in which all four parts of the choir enter simultaneously, a symbol of a universal sense of outrage which cannot be restrained by the polite conventions of normal choral writing. Any overlapping counterpoints here might obscure the words whose import is such that there must be absolute unanimity. Yet who can fail to be moved by the profoundly emotional quality of the harmonies at 'He was wounded for our transgressions', where the calculated dissonances vividly depict the pain while at the same time convey a deep compassion.

The chorus that follows (that gave poor Mr Janson such problems) is the first strict fugue to appear in the work. Earlier choruses may have seemed to be fugal in style but have not conformed to the academic rule that the first and third entries of the Subject should be in the Tonic key, the second and fourth entries in the Dominant.

A fugue such as this is essentially built up from two main components, the Subject and the Countersubject which, not surprisingly, are supposed to fit against each other. Any intervening passages not relevant to either will be called an Episode. The Subject is not invariably matched against its countersubject and may be treated in a number of ingenious ways – Inversion, turning it upside down; Augmentation, doubling the length of the notes; Diminution, halving the length of the notes; or even a combination of these. A commonly-used feature is a *stretto*, in which entries of the Subject overlap so closely that they crowd in before the Subject itself is completed.

In this chorus both Subject and Countersubject are settings of the same words, 'And with his stripes we are healed', the Subject symbolising pain and the Countersubject healing, the one angular and distorted, the other soothing.

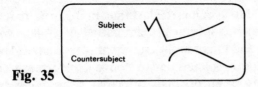

Fig. 35

The Exposition of the fugue, that is to say the first four entries of the subject, could be represented diagrammatically in this way:

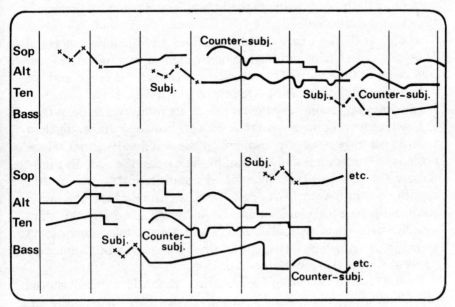

Fig. 36

Notice that although all four parts share the same material and indeed frequently imitate each other, no two parts ever coincide exactly into a unison; the texture is always interwoven. One wonders if Handel elected to set this portion of the text as a strict fugue so that it might be interpreted as a symbol of a severe discipline, flogging being commonplace in the army and navy at the time.

The subsequent chorus 'All we like sheep' sounds incongruously light-hearted after the agonised intensity of the previous four numbers. Only in its final page, 'And the Lord hath laid on him the iniquity of us all', do we find a worthy match to the true Passion music that has preceded it.

After a brief recitative in which the rhythm of the lash continues with cruel persistence, there is another strict fugue, 'He trusted in God'. The tone is derisive; it is the last time in the work that the choir is expected to play the specifically dramatic role of the '*turba*', the crowd. Although one might feel that anything so well organised as a fugue is hardly the best medium to convey the jeering cries of a rabble, it proves to be surprisingly effective, since one gets the impression of a leader setting passions aflame with some catch phrase which spreads its malice round about, being taken up by different voices in turn. It is worth noting that Bach uses a similar device, albeit with more dramatic brevity, in the St Matthew Passion for the words 'Let Him be crucified'.

The clear division between the religious and operatic aspects of Handel's genius is beautifully demonstrated in two recitatives and airs given to the tenor. 'Thy rebuke hath broken his heart' and the subsequent 'Behold and see' are profoundly spiritual. The sustained harmonies that accompany the recitative are indicative of deep feeling, while the ensuing air is far briefer than its operatic equivalent would ever have been. By comparison the two numbers that follow are not only less intensely felt but, in the case of the aria 'But thou didst not leave his soul in hell', so unashamedly lyrical that once again we are back in the world of opera. With a change of text the music could easily pass for a love song. (The justly popular 'Silent Worship' or 'Did you not see my Lady?' comes to mind as a fair comparison.) Compare its effortless lyricism with the rigid severity of 'Thou shalt break them', and the point is made.

Ending the second part of the oratorio with the 'Hallelujah' chorus must have presented Handel with something of an artistic problem. Especially as it is performed today, it has such an air of finality that one is still liable to feel that Part Three was added as an afterthought. It was a true touch of genius to follow it not with another chorus but an aria of sublime purity, 'I know that my Redeemer liveth'. The absence of any contrapuntal complexity in this aria is one of its most notable features; it is almost a duet for soprano and violins. After the explosively abrupt rhythms of the 'Hallelujah' chorus the long-drawn phrases give a wonderful effect of spaciousness. The one touch of pictorialism is disarmingly naive, the sinuous motion of the worms that 'destroy this body'; but even this is put to purely musical use once it has burrowed its way into our consciousness.

The close proximity of two such marvellously contrasted arias as 'Redeemer' and 'The trumpet shall sound' is evidence of Handel's prodigious fluency as a composer. However, it must be admitted that his muse flagged in the central section of the trumpet aria. The sequences trundle out in rather too pat a fashion, nor could he be bothered to write any but the most perfunctory of accompaniments. The passage is usually omitted from present-day performances, and it is possible that Handel wrote it more out of consideration for the trumpeter than for any high musical purpose. It is not surprising that after more than two weeks of incredible productivity even Handel began to tire, and it is generally accepted that the overall quality of the Third Part does not quite measure up to what has gone before. Fortunately the final Amen is magnificent, combining great contrapuntal skill with a feeling of sublime majesty. No chorus tenor who has sung the entry on a top A that comes eight bars from the end will ever forget the experience, yet it was an afterthought on Handel's part; originally he put it an octave lower where it would have made no memorable effect.

It would not be far wrong to say that the whole tradition of English choral singing was founded on Handel's great work, such was its popularity in later years. Under the quite mistaken idea that bigger equated with better, it was generally performed in a way that was quite alien to Handel's intentions, the most grotesque example of hyper-inflation occurring during the celebrations commemorating the centenary of the composer's death. To a choir of 2,000 was added an orchestra of 300 strings, 36 wind instruments, 12 horns, 12 trumpets and cornets, 9 trombones, 3 ophicleides and 9 serpents (now extinct), 3 drums and 6 side drums. The audience exceeded 10,000. A contemporary account records that

> The 'Hallelujah' Chorus could be distinctly heard half a
> mile from (the Crystal Palace), and its effect, as the sound
> floated on the wind was impressive beyond description, and
> sounded as if the nation were at prayers ... A burst of
> applause, which could no longer be restrained, attested, at
> its conclusion, the overpowering effect of this colossal
> interpretation of the 'Hallelujah' Chorus ... And the con-
> cluding 'Amen' was equal in all respects to the 'Hallelujah'
> and formed a fitting climax to the most impressive and
> exciting performance of the *Messiah* which has ever been
> witnessed.

Impressive and exciting it may have been, but it could scarcely have
been further from Handel's intentions. Unfortunately it set the
fashion; a series of Handel Festivals took place triennially at the
Crystal Palace; by 1923 the number of performers had grown to
4,000! Only in the last twenty-five years or so has it become increasingly acceptable to present Handel's music on the scale for which it
was originally conceived, and nowadays it is possible to attend performances or obtain recordings which, so far as scholarship can
ascertain, are true to the spirit of the original. Even this can cause
upsets, since in Handel's day it was quite accepted that singers should
add their own embellishments at suitable places, an idea which the
more conservative listener of today regards as offensive tampering
with the original.

12 __Notes for a novice_____

The performance of the *Messiah* so fired Mr Malcolm's enthusiasm that he decided that he could no longer remain a mere spectator. Although his voice was no more than adequate, he reckoned that he was no worse than some of the choir members who had clearly derived immense enjoyment from rehearsals and performance alike. Perhaps if he were to learn to read music, he might be able to pass the necessary audition; but was he too old to acquire the skill? With some apprehension he approached Mr Roberts.

'John, you know I've really got so much pleasure out of all your musical activities, it's been quite an eye-opener, or I suppose I should say ear-opener. The thing is, I'm beginning to feel I must join in. Saturday's *Messiah* quite bowled me over. Of course I've heard it before several times, but it made such a difference having been to most of the rehearsals and hearing it all come together. I know you're dreadfully busy, but could you possibly find time to give me some lessons – teach me enough to scrape through an audition for next season . . . I'd pay of course, I'd insist on that.'

The music master sighed a little heavily. 'I'd love to help, Keith, but honestly I'm up to my ears with work. Tell you what, though; young Tim, my assistant, is getting married soon and he'd be glad of a few extra quid. I'm sure he'd help you just as much as I ever could and you'd be doing him a favour. He's a nice lad and very bright.'

And so it was arranged. Once a week Mr Malcolm was to call on Tim to be initiated into the mysteries of music notation. Armed with a pencil and notebook, and feeling somewhat self-conscious at this reversion to school days, he duly presented himself for his first lesson. Tim gave him a cheerful welcome.

'Do you really want to start from scratch?' he asked, 'or are we reviving long-lost memories from childhood?'

Mr Malcolm looked a trifle sheepish. 'Well, I've been sitting in on rehearsals a lot and obviously I've got to know what music *looks* like, what with giving Miss Stebbing a hand and so on. But I really can't read it. I think you'd better assume that I know nothing.'

The two men settled down at a table. Tim pulled a sheet of totally blank paper off a pad.

'Well, the basics are quite simple really; it's when you get a lot of things going on at once that the brain gets bewildered. Let's start at the beginning, though. If a composer wants to put something down on paper, just a single note, say, what has he actually got to indicate? By the way, you don't mind if I call you Keith – Mr Malcolm sounds so formal.'

'Of course not. Umm – what's he got to indicate? Well, *which* note I suppose.'

'Certainly, but not just *which* note. He's got to show what its duration is, and how loud or soft it should be. Pitch, Duration, Volume, those really are the only three things that he needs to worry about.'

'I can't believe it's that simple. I took a look at the score of the *Messiah* and it seemed to be crammed with notes . . .'

'Of course it is – but that's because it shows everything that's going on at once. Look, let's start with a single line:

'How many notes do you reckon that shows?'

Keith gave an uncertain little laugh. 'Why, one I suppose.'

'No, three; one on the line, one above and one below.' He marked in three crosses:

'There's progress for you; before your very eyes you have the first phrase of "Three Blind Mice". If you want the next phrase, "See how they run", all we need do is to add one more line, so:

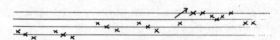

'Things get a bit more complicated now because the Farmer's Wife lives upstairs. Let's try four lines and see if they're enough:

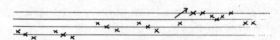

'You see there's a bigger gap between "they" and "all", so I've put a little arrow there to remind you. Now how many times is that last bit repeated?'

Keith, feeling rather as though he was back in the nursery, muttered tunelessly to himself,

> They all ran after the Farmer's Wife
> Who cut off their tails with a carving knife
> Did you ever see such a thing in your life
> As three blind mice . . .

'Er, three times.'

'Right,' said Tim, 'so I won't waste time writing it out twice more; I'll just put a bracket over it and put "3 times" and then we'll add the last bit.'

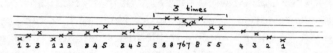

'Well now, we've solved the problem of Pitch, after a fashion, but before we go on do you notice anything unexpected? Just think about the lowest and highest notes of the tune . . .'

Keith hummed to himself, and then, rather like a poor singer trying his hand at some sort of vocal exercise, tried to pitch the notes for 'mice' and 'farmer'. It was not finely tuned but it served.

'They're the same aren't they – well, not exactly the same, but you know what I mean.'

'Yes, they're an octave apart, 'octave' coming from the *eight* notes of the scale. But what I wanted you to notice is that the bottom note is on a space while the top one is on a line. If you want to learn to sight-read, and that's what you're here for, you want to try to develop a sense of "interval" right from the start.'

'What do you mean by interval, exactly?'

'Measuring the distance between notes. Let's turn the mice upside down for the moment – call them Australian mice. . . . Suppose we write the tune this way, and I'll put figures over each note:

'Now the interval from note 1–2 is called a second, from note 1–3 is a third, 1–4 is a fourth, 1–5 a fifth and so on. With the set-up we've got here, if you go from space to space you get all the odd numbers, 1,3,5,7 while going from line to line you get the evens, 2,4,6,8. Some people think of this sort of grid thing as a ladder but that's dangerous because when you're climbing a ladder you only put your foot on the rungs, not in the spaces in between.

'Now four lines plus the spaces is all we need for a simple little tune like this but obviously we want a few more than that if we're going to cope with the Tchaikovsky Piano Concerto.'

Keith felt that he was about to take a rather giant step for himself if not for mankind. Tim suddenly drew what seemed an awful lot of lines and began to fill in crosses at a great rate, humming Tchaikovsky to himself the while:

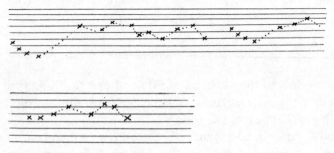

Fig. 37

'That's enough to go on with' he said, 'but you can see the sort of problem that's going to develop. It's jolly difficult to work out where you are when you're in the middle of the grid. Because you know the tune you can more or less follow it, but if you hadn't got that mental picture, you'd be floundering. Still, it's quite useful to imagine a great big grid like that because what we actually do is to pick just five lines out of the grid for any one instrument or voice. Instruments like the piano or the harp have two sets of five lines, one for each hand, and the organ has three, two for the hands and one for the feet. We call each set of five lines a "stave". Now the next problem is to identify which set of five lines we're going to use, so we have things called "clefs" – it's the French word for key, but that's confusing because there are several sorts of keys in music. Think of it as the key to a puzzle. If you're going to play a treble instrument like a violin or a flute or the right hand half of the piano, we use a squiggly sign like this: 𝄞 and we put it so that the loop goes round the second line up, indicating the note G.'

'Why not just write the letter G?' said Keith.

'Good question. Look I'll show you something rather interesting.'

Tim went over to the bookshelf, running his fingers along several shelves until, with a grunt of satisfaction, he pulled out a shabby volume.

'Have you ever heard of Gilles de Rais? One of Joan of Arc's generals he was; charming character; slaughtered about a hundred and thirty children over the years celebrating a sort of Black Mass. Anyway, here's his signature, and you'll see the G is an almost perfect treble clef.'

He held out the book to Keith and there it was:

'So there you are; stick Gilles de Rais' initial on to a five-line stave and we have a G clef, a G landmark if you like.'

And he quickly sketched in five lines with the familiar but hitherto rather meaningless symbol.

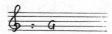

'Now we need only seven letters of the alphabet, A to G, so you can work them out for yourself; start from that G and work outwards.'

Feeling vaguely as though he was doing a new form of crossword puzzle, Keith began filling in letters.

'What happens if I want to go any lower than that D?' he asked. 'I seem to have run out of lines; how do I go down to A?'

'You simply borrow a line temporarily from the grid like this:' and Tim swiftly filled in the missing letters.

'The borrowed lines are called 'ledger' lines (you can spell it 'leger' if you like) and you can have as many as you want. Flute players get very good at spotting where they are even when the note looks as if it's stuck on a telegraph pole. See if you can work out this note.'

Somewhat laboriously Keith fingered his way up the 'telegraph pole', remembering that the note sitting on top of the stave would be G. With some satisfaction he ultimately said 'It's an A.'

'Right,' said Tim; 'well done. But your flute player, remembering that tip I gave you about the octave, would instantly spot the fourth ledger *line* as the octave above the top *space* G and think of it automatically as one more than an octave, and you're right – that would be A.

'Now if you want to use a whole lot of the lower notes, which you do if you play the cello or the bassoon, (or with your left hand on the piano) you use a different set of five lines from the grid, and the one that gets identified as a landmark is the F an octave and one note below our G clef. The sign used to show this is a bit confusing because it looks like a C back to front with a couple of dots after it.

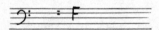

'The two dots are placed each side of the F line. The way I teach my junior class how to remember it's an F is to draw a rather elaborate capital letter in this style:

'then I smooth it out like this:

'There's one clef called the C clef and that's a rather interesting one because you don't always put it on the same line of the grid – or so it seems. Actually it *is* the same line because it's always the line for middle C, but you can adjust its position on the grid like this. Viola parts, which use the middle area of the piano a lot, are written with the C clef on the middle line of five:

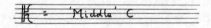

'but when you play an instrument like the tenor trombone the patch of the grid you're most likely to use would be around here:

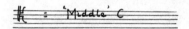

so middle C comes on the second line from the top. In fact these areas all overlap so that the principle of borrowing a bit from an adjacent "stave" becomes quite easy to understand.'

And here Tim ruled out something that looked a bit like a staircase:

Fig. 38

'Now if you imagine the grid continues indefinitely either up or down, you can see that we might have very high notes written with lots of ledger-lines up above or very low notes with lots of ledger-lines down below, but the area covered here is about all that's needed for choral music in particular and nearly all the first music that was written down was for voices. Back in the Middle Ages they used a simplified and less accurate "grid", and in Elizabethan times they used six lines to a stave instead of five, but you should have got the basic idea by now.

'Anyway, that's looked after one problem, indicating the Pitch of a note. Now we come to something rather more complicated and that's the Duration. Because music moves in a time dimension, we have to know how long a note is supposed to last, not in terms of seconds or fractions of a second, but in relation to its neighbours. Take "Good King Wenceslas" for instance; all the first syllables are equal in length:

Good King Wenceslas looked OUT

until that word OUT, which is twice as long as the ones before it. Then we have all 'equals' again until STE-PHEN, and that's *two* syllables that are twice as long.

'Now my children in class always think notation is going to be a bit boring so I try to get them interested by talking about frogspawn and tadpoles – much more fun.'

Keith couldn't help laughing at the change of tack; boyhood memories of splashing about at the edge of a pond with a little fishing net on a slender bit of bamboo came flooding into his mind.

'IN THE BEGINNING', said Tim solemnly, imitating the rather pompous tones of the school chaplain, 'IN THE BEGINNING came the egg.' And he drew one:

o

'And the egg was without form and void, except that it was worth four beats because I say so.'

'What do you mean, four *beats*?'

'Don't ask awkward questions; attend. Lo and behold it came to pass that one day the egg wanted to move, so it grew a tail.' Tim added a tail of sorts to his original drawing.

ρ

'Now this is where the tadpole bit comes in because what I do is fill in the "head", like this:

♩

'Then, say I to the kids, the tadpole wants to swim, so it gives a flick of its tail:

♪

'and when it wants to swim faster still, it gives a double flick:

♬

or even a triple one:

♬

'While they're swimming about, tadpoles are liable to meet other tadpoles, and when they do they link tails like this:

⌐⌐

'Someone like David Attenborough would probably say they're getting up to something fearfully rude, but I don't think so, because sometimes they link up in threes: ⌊⌊⌋ or fours: ⌊ ⌊ ⌊ ⌊ and they can also join together when they're swimming along quite fast, like this:

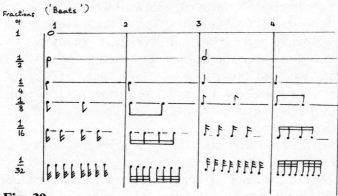

'That last group is really wild isn't it . . .'

Although Keith wasn't quite sure if he was being got at, he did realise that what Tim was doing was drawing symbols which he'd seen many times on sheets of music but whose significance he'd never really understood.

Tim went on: 'Once I've got the little blighters' interest by all this waffle about tadpoles, it's quite easy to steer them back to reality and make a chart like this:

Fig. 39

'You see that the "tails" can either be below or above the "head", that's purely a matter of convenience.'

'What are the fractions for?' asked Keith. 'I don't quite see the logic of that.'

'Well it isn't awfully logical in a way because if we're thinking in terms of "beats", it seems awfully silly to have the symbol for four beats, the "egg", counting as the "whole" of which the smaller subdivisions are then fractions. It dates back to a very long time ago when early music was written in "long" units only. In fact my "egg" note is called a semi-breve, half-a-breve, because there used to be a note twice as long called a breve, which in our terms would be worth eight beats. Since breve means short it seems dafter still to call the longest possible written note a "short", but I tell my kids it was because the monks were fearfully slow on the uptake and it made them feel better to *think* it was a short note even though it took them ages to work it out. I don't think that's exactly gospel truth, but it seems to amuse them; at least they remember it.'

'What are the other notes called?' said Keith.

'Well I'd rather you understood the principles than tried to remember the names but the "half" notes are called minims, the "quarter" notes crotchets, the "eighth" notes quavers, the "sixteenth" notes semi-quavers, and then it goes mad with demi-semi-quavers and even hemi-demi-semi-quavers, which, I tell my class, are the fastest swimming tadpoles in the world, Olympic medallists every one. . . . Actually, the Americans use the fractional terms, "half", "quarter" and so on; it's much more logical. But even that sounds a bit silly when you get to a "sixty-fourth" note.

'Where the fractions come into their own is when a composer wants to show how *many* of what *kind* of beats there are in a bar. For instance waltzes have three beats in a bar, three "quarters", so that's exactly what you put at the beginning of a waltz, 3/4. "Good King Wenceslas" has four beats in a bar, four "quarters" so its time-signature, as it's called, is 4/4. A tune like "Greensleeves" is interesting; it could be thought of as lots of 1 2 3's, like a very quick waltz, but it flows more naturally in six.'

Tim sang it gently, counting 1 2 3 4 5 6, 1 2 3 4 5 6, 1 2 3 4 5 6, 1 2 3 4 5 6 as he went along.

'Since the notes are not all that slow, sort of medium fast tadpoles, we use the eighth note or quaver as the main unit, so the time-signature will be 6/8. You can have quite odd-looking time-signatures though; for instance hymns are often written in minims, half-notes, so "Hark! The Herald Angels Sing" will have a time-signature of 4/2, four half-notes to each bar. Of course modern composers often go in for irregular pulses and you may find things like 7/8 or 11/16 cropping up; just remember that the upper figure tells you how many and the lower figure what kind.

'Right; we know how to show the pitch, we know how to show what the main pulse of the music is going to be (how many beats in a bar) and we know how to show the duration of individual notes. The next step is to find out how to string different rhythms together so as to make a whole tune. Let's start with good old Wenceslas shall we; it's a nice easy one.'

Tim started to hum the tune, jotting down the notes as he did so. It meant that he had to take the melody rather slowly because it took time for even his practised hand to make each note-head and add its tail; but after a moment or two he had written a line like this:

Fig. 40

'The first four bars come twice, don't they', he said as he surveyed the finished tune. 'So I drew what we call a double bar and put those two little dots there. That means 'repeat', and you go back to the beginning in this case, or, if it happens later on in a piece, back to the preceding pair of dots. It saves a lot of trouble, and in things like classical minuets and trios you'll also find an instruction at the end of the trio saying *D.C. senza repetizione* which is Italian for "From the top" – *Da Capo* – "without repeats".

'All we've got to do now is to colour it a bit by putting in some expression marks. *Crescendo* means "getting louder". *Decrescendo* or *Diminuendo* means "getting softer". They're such long words to write down that we usually abbreviate them to *cresc.* or *dim.* or, and this is much more common, we draw a symbol like this ————— or this ———————— , and I needn't tell you which is which. Then there are all sorts of other words like *forte* for loud, *piano* for soft, *mezzo-forte* for medium loud, or the "-issimos", *fortissimo* for very loud, *pianissimo* for very soft. But again, we mostly use abbreviations like *pp, p, mp, mf, f* and *ff*. *Più* means more and *Meno* means less, so let's dress up the tune a bit and give it the full treatment – much more than is needed really, but it'll show you what could be done.'

Rather like a make-up girl applying deft touches of colour to an actor's face, Tim went along the line of music flicking in the various symbols to show what, he said, 'are properly called *dynamics*'.

Fig. 41

'What do *rit.* and *allarg.* mean?' asked Keith, 'and what's that eye-brow thing in the last bar?'

'Oh, that means pause, and the sign may very well represent an eye and an eyebrow, meaning "Watch Out!" As for *rit.* and *allarg.*, they're just abbreviations for *ritardando*, getting slower, and *allargando*, broadening. There are masses of Italian words like that; you can find them in any glossary of musical terms.'

'One thing you haven't mentioned', said Keith, 'is the sort of cross thing; I think it's called a sharp, isn't it?'

'Oh yes. Well that shows the key the piece is in – in this case, G major. It doesn't affect singers so much really because they make the necessary adjustment by ear. But if you play that tune on the piano it means you've got to remember to play a black note each time you get to F; otherwise it'd sound a bit peculiar.' And Tim played the third bar of the tune with an F natural (♮) instead of the sharp (♯) and it did indeed sound a bit odd.

Tim cleared his throat; he seemed to have been doing a lot of talking.

'I tell you what,' he went on. 'I gather you're partly here because you enjoyed our *Messiah* so much. I'll jot down the opening bars of a few of the choruses and see if you recognise what they are.'

He pulled a sheet of manuscript paper out of a drawer – 'Don't want to go on ruling lines all night' – and started to write. As he scribbled the notes down, he gave a sort of running commentary.

Fig. 42

'I haven't said anything about those little squiggly worms in the second bar. They're called rests, and they just mean "Shut up", but they show you how many beats you've got to shut up for – in this case the second and third. One useful tip when you're sight-reading is to work out which note of the scale you're starting on. The key signature tells us that we're in G major, so starting from G as the home-base, you can see the tune starts on the fifth note of the scale. Go on, have a go.'

'But I don't know where G is', said Keith with a slight air of apology for not being able to pluck the vital but elusive note out of the air.

'That doesn't matter,' said Tim cheerfully. 'Pitch is a very relative thing at this stage. Just find a comfortable note, and sing it a few times to get it fixed in your mind. Then go up five to find your starting-point.'

Keith made a few tentative attempts to find some sort of a tonal haven to which he could return in times of stress, and then started to sing after a fashion.

'Why, it's "For unto us",' he said with a note of satisfaction.

'There you are,' said Tim. 'I told you you'd be able to do it. Now have a try at this.'

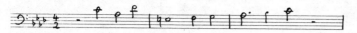

Fig. 43(a)

'What note do you start on?'

'A.'

'No; you're still thinking in the treble clef; I put this one in the bass to catch you out. Remember those two dots to give you your land-mark of F.'

Keith hummed his way up from an imagined F, climbing through five notes of the scale.

'Now drop a third, and then go back to one higher than you started from.' Though still feeling self-conscious at having to perform unaided, Keith groped his way through this a little more successfully than poor Janson had back in 1741, but then he did have the advan-tage of having heard it rehearsed a number of times.

'It's "And with his stripes",' he said. 'You can really see the shape of the phrase can't you, with that swoop down to the word "stripes".'

'That's exactly the idea of what I mean about learning to recognise intervals,' said Tim approvingly. 'It really doesn't take long for the eye to spot what a third or a fifth looks like, and once you get those distances fixed in your mind, the voice learns to place them accu-rately.

'What's that dot thing like a full stop in the third bar?' said Keith.

'Oh, that's very convenient', said Tim. 'It adds half the value of the preceding note symbol whatever it may be. In this case we want a minim, or two-beat note, to be lengthened by half, making it into a three-beat note. Now, we could do it by writing in the third beat and joining it to the first note with a curved line called a "tie" to show that you don't actually play it but give it the extra value.

Fig. 43(b)

'But that takes time and space; it's much less trouble for the composer just to put a dot in.'

Fig. 43(c)

'Incidentally, talking of time, I see it's getting on a bit; would you like to stop now or shall we do one more, this time not from Messiah, so as to test you a little bit more severely? No clues given, but watch my hand as I'm writing and see if you can build up an idea of the tune as we go along.'

Keith was again impressed at the speed with which Tim was able to put down the notes, almost it seemed, without thought.

Fig. 44

When they were only half way through, Keith had confidently asserted that it was 'Rule Britannia'. Nevertheless Tim continued to write the tune out to its final cadence, pointing out the occasional rests, and indicating how easy it was to cope with the little runs which nearly always moved in scale-like progressions.

'The only sizeable jumps,' said Tim, 'I've marked with a pair of crosses, and what you want to do there is to remember the tip about octaves, and how if the bottom note of an octave is on a space then the top note will be on a line and vice versa.

'So what you do is to go *down* a line in your mind and then *up* an octave, so that you have a *"thinks"* note to help you span the gap. Actually Arne, the composer, puts it in for you first time round.

'It's very helpful in the early stages to learn to put in stepping-stones to help you on your way. But one thing I would stress; if you want to become a good reader, always start by reading things you actually *know*, so that you have the right answer in your head, rather than groping around vaguely and getting muddled and insecure. However, because you know the tune, don't cheat and sing it by ear. Sing it closely following every note, looking at all the details of how the rhythm is shown and so on; that way you'll teach yourself to associate sight and sound accurately.'

Already Keith was beginning to feel a little more hopeful that with a bit of practice this reading lark mightn't be quite so difficult as he had imagined it to be.

And neither is it. Obviously in a first lesson everything tends to be simplified; but a foundation has been laid, establishing two fundamentals, that one should know where one is within the scale, and that one should develop a feeling for intervals. A simple exercise to cultivate this essential skill is to start from the first note of any scale that suits your voice and, returning to base each time, go in turn to each note of the scale, naming the interval as you do so.

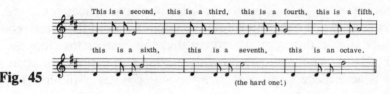

Fig. 45

Then do the same thing working down from the top note to this
pattern:

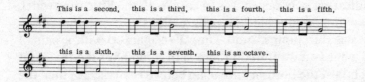

After this feels secure, break up the pattern at random; it is the best
way to develop the ability to imagine the sound of an interval when
confronted with it on the printed page.

Naturally the rhythmic problems of music notation have been
sketched in only very briefly so far. A way of developing a better
understanding of more complex rhythms is to find a piece of music
that is familiar and then to write it down in alternative notation.
Notation and tempo are closely related; it is possible to write down a
tune in several ways that will all *sound* the same though they *look*
different; an adjustment of tempo will even things out. Here is the
start of one of Mozart's most famous piano sonatas, the one that got
landed with the unfortunate title 'In an Eighteenth-century
drawing-room.'

Written this way it would *sound* exactly the same:

Or even like this:

The choice of notation is partly a matter of convenience; yet to the
performing musician the interpretative implications of the three versions above are different. Paradoxically, the one in the 'longest'
notion, No. 3, would be played with the most fire, since the word
Presto is here more significant than the actual notes, although they

too would have a stylistic implication too subtle to go into at this stage
of our musical journey.

By way of an exercise in developing reading skills, here are a
number of well-known themes which I have left unidentified. See if
you can discover what they are; you may be surprised how easily you
begin to comprehend their shape even though, without further guidance, the rhythms may have to be guessed rather than accurately
interpreted.

Fig. 46(a)

(b)

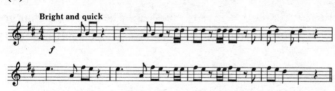

(c)

This is easier to read when it is written out in notes of twice the value:

The sound is the same if the tempo is adjusted.

Pathway to music

(d)

(e)

(f)

(a) J. S. Bach, 'Jesu, Joy of Man's Desiring'; (b) Handel, 'Hallelujah' chorus; (c) Beethoven, Symphony no. 5, slow movement; (d) Tchaikovsky, Piano Concerto no. 1, main theme; (e) Dvořák, Symphony no. 5, 'From the New World', slow movement; (f) Rakhmaninov, Piano Concerto no. 2, main theme.

140

Part Three

13 __Concert night__

They had reached the outskirts of London and progress was slow as they seemed to crawl from one red traffic light to another. John and Keith sat in the front seats of the suitably-named Maestro – 'Does my morale good as a conductor every time I get in', John had said jokingly – while behind, Sally and Terry conversed in discreet whispers. Both had been invited to the concert to mark the end of their days with Mr Roberts's youth orchestra, a small but suitable reward for all the work they'd put in in their spare time. For Keith it was, surprisingly, his first visit to the Royal Festival Hall, and he was looking forward to the concert with an enthusiasm he certainly would never have dreamed of some months previously; but after the undoubted enjoyment he had derived from his growing involvement with the music at John's school, he now felt he was more than ready to experience a public concert with a fully professional orchestra.

'Is there anything I should know about the music in advance?' he asked at one particularly long wait at a major traffic intersection.

'Well, first on the menu is Mozart's Overture to *The Marriage of Figaro*. I always like the opera's subtitle; it's called *La folle journée*, the mad day, because all the action takes place within twenty-four hours. But wouldn't "Crazy Day" be a marvellous title for a musical!'

'Starring Gene Kelly as Figaro I suppose,' said Keith, enjoying the moment of fantasy.

'Funny you should say that, because one of the singers in the first performance was an Irish tenor called Michael Kelly; he wrote some quite extensive memoirs which give us a very graphic description of the rehearsals under Mozart's direction. They'll probably be quoted in the programme notes with a bit of luck, so you'll be able to read them for yourself.'

'Presumably the Overture contains quite a few of the tunes from the opera?'

'No; that was more of a nineteenth-century idea; I expect you're thinking in particular of Gilbert and Sullivan where, much as they do in a modern musical, they plug the hit tunes of the show right from the beginning – a sort of musical brain-washing. There's a classic instance of that in the overture to Humperdinck's opera *Hansel and Gretel*, absolutely enchanting stuff; but some of the Wagner overtures, like *The Mastersingers*, fall into the same category, giving the audience a sort of conducted tour of the principal themes so that they'll recognise them later. Mozart's approach is quite different; he will certainly set the *mood* of the opera, but he seldom anticipates any of the arias. He does in *Seraglio* but that's exceptional. Come to think of it, there is a sort of preview in the overture to *Cosi fan tutte*. It's only a few chords, but they do appear near the end of the opera as a setting of those actual words. And then of course the trombones at the start of the *Don Giovanni* overture give us an ominous forecast of the terrific moment when the statue of the man Don Giovanni has killed arrives at the feast in the last act. Have you ever thought how Mozart would have loved the cinema? His operas are full of situations that only film could do adequate justice to.'

Weaving his way through a tortuous diversion caused by some mysterious excavations in the centre of the high road, John continued his dissertation untroubled by the rain-splashed cars that seemed to be coming at him from several directions at once.

'The *Figaro* Overture starts very quietly, with swift bustling phrases that suggest the early morning activity in the Count's household as the servants prepare for a very busy day. That's one of the remarkable features of the opera; it focusses on the lower orders rather than the ruling classes; the hero is the Count's valet, not the Count; the heroine is the Countess's maid, not the Countess. Some of the Viennese aristocracy were quite upset by that and the opera was much more successful in Prague where there was a more prosperous middle class. But Mozart knew only too well what it was like to be a rather lowly paid employee in a Count's household (Count Colleredo his employer was also an Archbishop incidentally, but certainly didn't behave like one) and I always feel that Mozart must have particularly enjoyed working on an opera in which servants outwit their masters.'

Approaching the river from the south they caught a quick glimpse of Big Ben as they swung right towards the concert-hall. Safely parked, it was only a short walk to the main entrance, delightfully situated so as to face one of the most famous views in London. As they entered the main foyer, Keith was impressed with the feeling of light and space. The auditorium itself was not visible, but the atmosphere was welcoming, conveying clearly that music was something to lift the spirit. A green-uniformed attendant directed them up a short flight of stone stairs at the top of which was an attractive bookstall, its glass-fronted cases well stocked with a wide range of books on musical topics. John slowed his pace, glancing enviously at the display.

'I always feel I could spend a small fortune here,' he said; 'still, it's nice even to browse.'

Sally and Terry had gone ahead to buy programmes and soon the four of them were mounting a green-carpeted staircase to a higher level. The programme, unashamedly popular, had drawn a good crowd, and when they entered the hall itself it seemed to be more than three-quarters full, even with some ten minutes to go. Keith found the design of the building fascinating, the boxes at the sides looking like half-opened drawers in a giant wardrobe, the forest of organ pipes behind the platform a pleasingly abstract yet functional pattern that drew the eye compulsively. Every seat appeared to have a good view, and there was a reassuring lack of pretentiousness that suggested that music was the first priority in the architect's mind. They soon found their seats and, after the usual dithering as to who should sit where, settled comfortably into their places. Keith, determined to show himself a keen student, started to study the programme notes.

'Look,' said John, pointing to a paragraph half way down the page; 'there's a quotation from Kelly's *Reminiscences*. It really takes you back to what the original rehearsals must have been like.'

Keith started to read:

> I remember at the first rehearsal of the full band, Mozart was on the stage with his crimson fur-lined mantle and gold-laced cocked hat, giving the time of the music to the orchestra. Benucci, playing the part of Figaro, sang the famous aria '*Non più andrai*' with the greatest animation and power of voice. I was standing close to Mozart, who, *sotto voce*, was repeating, 'Bravo! Bravo! Benucci'; and when Benucci came to the fine passage, '*Cherubino, alla vittoria, alla gloria militar*,' which he gave out with stentorian lungs, the effect was electricity itself, for the whole of the performers on the stage, and those in the orchestra, as if actuated by one feeling of delight, vociferated 'Bravo! Bravo! Maestro! Viva, viva, grande Mozart.' Those in the

orchestra I thought would never have ceased applauding, by beating the bows of their violins against the music-desks. The little man acknowledged, by repeated obeisances, his thanks for the distinguished mark of enthusiastic applause bestowed upon him.

Somehow Keith had never thought of Mozart as being particularly small, and was touched to discover another phrase of Kelly's:

I shall never forget his little animated countenance when lighted up with the glowing rays of genius; it is as impossible to describe it as it would be to paint sunbeams.

By now the members of the orchestra were filing into place on the platform, their instruments gleaming beneath the brilliant lighting. Quite a few seats were left vacant, the conductor properly preferring to use a relatively small orchestra to do justice to the transparency of Mozart's scoring. The familiar sounds of tuning began, not quite so raucously as when Keith had first experienced them at the school rehearsals, and then, as if on some hidden signal, the players suddenly became silent, filling the hall with a sense of expectancy. A curtain to the left of the stage was swiftly drawn aside, and the leader, violin and bow in hand, stepped briskly on to the platform; having acknowledged the applause with a bow, he sat down, surveying his colleagues with a searching glance to see that all was in order. For a second time the curtain was pulled open by the backstage manager and the conductor, a commanding figure made his way between the first and second violins to his rostrum.

The welcoming applause died down. Glancing round, the great man saw an embarrassed couple hastening to their seats, the last to be admitted before the doors were firmly closed. (Any further latecomers would have to wait outside until the conclusion of the overture which, however, they could at least watch on monitor screens provided by a thoughtful management.)

With a gesture of authority that not only alerted the strings but silenced the few suppressed coughs that came from the audience, the conductor raised his baton, exchanged a quick glance with the leader, and then, with a tiny but meticulous beat, launched the overture on its way. Novice though he was, Keith realised at once that here was a precision and control that the band of young players he had listened

to so often could not hope to emulate. There was a delightful crisp-
ness about the wind entries, a thrilling attack in the more brilliant
passages and a remarkable range of tone colour. Above all, he was
impressed by the absolute unanimity of approach which made it seem
as though the orchestra was a single instrument being 'played' by the
conductor, so that every important strand was revealed with absolute
clarity.

The word Overture is susceptible to almost as many different
interpretations as is the generic term Symphony; indeed there was a
time when the two were virtually interchangeable. A composer of
Handel's day would have been equally happy to call the introduction
to a choral work an Overture or a Sinfonia, and both terms are to be
found in different editions of his *Messiah*. The word is derived from
the French *Ouverture*, literally an 'opening', presumably of curtains
in the theatre. But as the symphony proper developed into an
extended concert-piece in several movements, the overture came to
be associated more consistently with the stage and in particular the
opera. Since opera-houses were also used for the staging of spoken
drama, it was desirable to give the orchestra something to do on
non-operatic nights. It was in this way that overtures and *entr'acte*
music became a feature of theatrical entertainment. Although a great
deal of the musical fare provided for such occasions was probably
rather second rate, even the greatest composers did not scorn com-
missions to write incidental music. Beethoven provided notable
scores for Goethe's *Egmont*, Collin's *Coriolan* and several other
lesser-known plays, while Schubert's beguiling music to *Rosamunde*
has understandably continued to delight audiences long after the
trashy play for which it was put together has been forgotten. (I say
'put together' rather than composed, since to save time and trouble
he partly used music he had already written for a melodrama called
The Magic Harp.)

During the nineteenth century the concert overture began to
develop as a form independent from the theatre. Such works were
often inspired by literature or legend; but on occasion, a personal
experience could evoke a musical reaction. On 7 August 1829,
Mendelssohn wrote from Scotland to his family: '. . . in order to make
you understand how extraordinarily the Hebrides affected me, the
following came into my mind there.' And at the foot of the letter he
sketched in remarkable detail the music which in due course was to

develop into the justly popular 'Hebrides' Overture, even indicating the orchestration that he had in mind. It was an example of truly spontaneous inspiration which the subsequent application of conscious skills turned into a work of genius. Although prompted by an experience that fired his imagination, the 'Hebrides' Overture is virtually a symphonic movement with clearly defined first and second subject material and a tautly controlled Development. In this respect it is quite different from such a work as Smetana's *Vltava*, also inspired by nature it is true, but essentially episodic in character as it describes the progress of a great river from its source in the mountains to the majestic width it reaches beyond the rapids of St John. While it could be argued that *Vltava* has a suggestion of Rondo form in that one theme recurs a number of times throughout, it could more suitably be described as a symphonic poem.

The symphonic poem, an extensive elaboration of the overture, was initially developed by Liszt; it was obviously a form that appealed to him since he wrote no less than thirteen over a period of more than thirty years. He was inspired by poems (Byron, Victor Hugo, Lamartine, Schiller), legends (Orpheus, Prometheus) or drama (Hamlet). Even his two symphonies stem from literary sources, Goethe's *Faust* and Dante's *Divine Comedy*, and it was this conscious attempt to fuse music and literature that is one of the great distinguishing features of Romantic, as opposed to Classical, music. Schumann, Berlioz and Tchaikovsky all sought to find through literature some solution to the problems which the gradual disintegration of symphonic form brought in its wake. It was felt that if the audience could identify themes with 'characters', as in a play or poem, the comprehension of their deployment in a large-scale composition would be simplified. The aesthetic problem that arose was caused by the essentially different ways in which music and narrative develop. All large-scale musical forms depend on recognition through repetition; the repetition need not be slavish, and indeed the very character of a salient theme may be fundamentally changed, as we have seen. But without some such landmarks the listener is lost, as Wagner very well realised when, in his grand design of the *Ring* cycle of operas, he used so-called '*Leitmotifs*' as constantly recurring features. Without them the music would be in danger of becoming a formless mass. However, when we turn to narrative, repetition serves as a brake to progress. It was for this reason that such literary-minded composers as Liszt and Berlioz became obsessed by the idea of the *transformation* of themes as opposed to their repetition. The very word transformation implies progression from one state to another; in 'transforming' a theme from brashly heroic to tenderly sentimental, Liszt is, as it were, taking his hero-figure from the battlefield to the bedchamber. As long as we recognise the theme as being the same in essence, albeit different in behaviour and circumstance, the fusion between the literary concept of narrative and the musical concept of development is achieved. Even so, music and literature are not wholly compatible. Dukas' *Sorcerer's Apprentice* is perhaps the supremely successful example of story-telling in music without the aid of any narrator, but despite its brilliantly skilful use of the orchestra, its musical content is strictly limited, being roughly comparable to a Teddy Bears' Picnic supplied by Fortnum and Mason.

One need hardly say that Shakespeare was a vital source of inspiration to the Romantic composers, and it is interesting to note that virtually all the most successful attempts to treat his plays musically do so in the most general terms. Innumerable operatic versions failed dismally, only Verdi in his late maturity finding a matching genius in *Otello* and *Falstaff*. Paradoxically, the most satisfying way of relating Shakespeare to music seemed to be to dispense with the text entirely.

Tchaikovsky described his *Romeo and Juliet* as a Fantasy-Overture rather than a symphonic poem, largely because the narrative element is almost entirely absent. Here indeed the audience can identify themes with characters, the solemn organ-like theme for Friar Laurence, the impassioned melody that symbolises Romeo's love for Juliet, the very audible clash of arms that represents the fights between Montagues and Capulets, the soothing croon of the nurse, the tragic funeral procession at the end. But in terms of the play, the order of events is chaotic, deliberately so, since Tchaikovsky is working to the principles of musical construction, not stage drama. The same applies to the less well-known and wrongfully underrated *Hamlet* overture, as it does to the overture Berlioz wrote based on *King Lear*.

The intrinsic danger of setting too much store on narrative in music is best illustrated by Richard Strauss's *Don Quixote*, a work in which the Don is portrayed by a solo cello while the role of Sancho Panza is given to a viola. If one were to listen to this work without knowing anything of its genesis, it would surely be quite baffling. Certainly there would be passages that might have an overwhelming effect of power or beauty; but the extremely episodic nature of the music could only cause confusion if one did not know what it was supposedly describing as specific events in a story. Without a guide book in the form of a comprehensive programme-note, one is lost.

It has often been maintained that programmatic music is the easiest of all for the novice listener to come to terms with; but this holds true only if he has a clear idea of the nature of the story and the sequence of events. Once the thread is lost the effort to regain contact can distract his entire attention from the music.

I once, as an experiment, devised a totally false narrative to accompany the opening few pages of Elgar's *Falstaff*. It fitted perfectly down to the smallest detail, yet bore no resemblance to the images that Elgar had in mind according to his own description. My purpose was not malicious; I simply wanted to show the fallibility of music when it comes to portraiture. A noble theme, splendidly scored, will serve as well to depict Prince Hal, one's first glimpse of Conway Castle, or H.M.S. *Victory* setting sail from Portsmouth Harbour. Once the initial image is planted in the mind, our imaginations will fill in the details. How wise Beethoven was to preface the slow movement of his Pastoral Symphony with the words 'More an expression of feeling than a painting'. And is it not true in all honesty that those brief passages that can literally be identified as the song of cuckoo, quail or nightingale (near the end of the movement) are musically inferior to the rest? They may have a certain naive charm, but their intrusion into the concert-hall makes them seem like toys rather than birds. It is interesting to note that Mozart did not make a similar miscalculation, for in *The Magic Flute* he indeed gives Papageno, the bird-catcher, a toy set of pipes to lure his prey; and because it *is* a toy, and seen to be one, we are enchanted.

Warm applause greeted the overture. The conductor bowed a couple of times and then left the stage. A number of extra players made their way to their seats while with such magical efficiency that Keith hardly saw how it was done, a concert grand piano was wheeled into place. He noted that it seemed that the conductor was going to stand beyond the piano, in close proximity to the viola section, and he asked John why he should thus be banished to a position where few of the audience could see him.

'It's a matter of visibility', said John. 'With the lid of the piano fully raised, it would be very hard for a lot of the players to see the beat. Mind you, why they don't make perspex lids for grand pianos I don't know; I always think it'd make life easier for everyone involved; perhaps it might affect the tone quality though.'

The concerto was Rakhmaninov's second, which Keith knew in various corrupted and commercialised versions but which he had never heard in a proper performance. Hastily he skimmed through the programme notes. There appeared to be a rather strange story attached to the work. Apparently Rakhmaninov had suffered a severe loss of confidence amounting to a virtual breakdown after a catastrophic first performance of his Symphony No. 1. For a time the well-springs of creativity completely dried up and he felt that his future as a composer was doomed. Meanwhile he established a successful career as a conductor, principally in the opera-pit. Finally, on the advice of friends, he sought help from a Dr Nikolay Dahl, a medically trained hypnotist. In true Hollywood style Dr Dahl convinced Rakhmaninov that his powers would be restored and, within a remarkably short time, the composer was able to resume his activities, dedicating the Second Piano Concerto to the good doctor as an indication of his gratitude.

Strangely enough, the first movement was the last to appear; the work was first heard on 15 December 1900 in truncated form with the second and third movements only. Its success was enough to give Rakhmaninov the encouragement he needed to go ahead with the first movement, a task he accomplished so successfully that one would never believe that it was the last to be written. (Apart from the somewhat melodramatic touch of the hypnotist, a rather similar episode occurred with the Schumann piano concerto whose first and third movements were written as independent works. It was his wife, Clara, who persuaded Schumann to write a central movement, thereby creating a genuine three-movement concerto.)

A mounting crescendo of applause aroused Keith from his study of the programme and he looked up to see the soloist and conductor weaving a deliberate path through the now rather more closely-packed ranks of violins. The pianist sat down, made a minute adjustment to the height of the stool, and then rubbed his hands together as though to ensure that every muscle was relaxed and flexible. A profound stillness enveloped the hall; the best part of three thousand people seemed to freeze into total silence awaiting the magical first chords with which the concerto begins.

It would be hard to find a more eloquent demonstration of the power of harmony to increase or lessen tension than the opening chords of this famous work. The outer limits remain the same, C at the top, F at the bottom; but the inner notes change, adding varying degrees of dissonance as the chords grow in intensity. Eight times the bell-like tones ring out before the inevitable break-out from so conscious a restraint occurs. The strongly marked octaves with which the pattern is finally broken prove to be the first indication of the most important thematic unit in the whole movement:

Fig. 47

Add one more note to this relatively conventional idea and you have what is normally described as a 'motto' theme, one which reappears in numerous guises even though it may not necessarily deserve the distinction of being called the First Subject. That undoubtedly comes on the strings, a great, broad swinging tune that the pianist accompanies with swirling figures that suggest waves beating upon a rocky shore. (See p. 140, f.)

The tune is notable for its length, as well as for the fact that it remains the exclusive property of the orchestra. Nowhere in the concerto does the soloist actually play this splendid opening theme, a precedent Rakhmaninov may have borrowed quite unwittingly from Mozart's concerto in the same key, however different the idiom of the two works may be. But after sixteen bars the cellos lead off with what might be called the second main paragraph of the tune, and this the soloist is allowed to get his hands on in due course. It is a fine melodic extension of the 'motto' theme, as can be seen by placing them side by side:

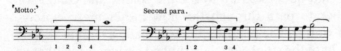

Fig. 48

and it is this phrase which in due course allows the soloist to escape from the role of accompanist and take over the lead. It is a lyrical moment that is destined to have a very brief life, for after a mere eight bars there is a noticeable acceleration of tempo and some brilliantly glittering figuration from the piano leads to a sudden loud outburst from the orchestra which is rapidly quelled to make way for the memorable Second Subject. This is a perfect example of the type of tune that is adored by the public and scorned by the critics. Both views are defensible. That legendary creature the 'man-in-the-street' responds to the overt passion in the music, a passion tinged with the melancholy that one associates with a love that once burned bright but which is now only a memory; the critic deplores the tendency of the music to be a series of journeys to nowhere, the melodies returning all too often to their point of departure, despite the appearance of chromatic wanderings. The cadences are drawn out to the point of self-indulgence, although it is perhaps the feeling of sinking into the eiderdown comfort of predictable harmony that gives the uncritical ear such reassurance. Whichever view one takes, there is no denying the richness of the piano writing nor its perfect suitability to the keyboard. The Second Subject ends with an ethereal ascent into the upper register of the piano whose outline is sympathetically traced by the violins to beautiful effect. Suddenly the spell is broken and the piano part races away into a clatter of notes which produces a distinctly ponderous reaction from the heavy brass. (It is a distorted version of the four-note 'motto' theme, enough, perhaps, to remind us of its existence since it is due to play an increasingly important part in the developments that lie ahead.)

For a few bars the soloist is silent. Violas offer a somewhat gloomy version of the original First Subject, its heroic mood now suppressed, while fragmentary allusions to the 'motto' theme crop up in the lower strings, or, more optimistically, in the flutes.

Fig. 49

As soon as the soloist re-enters there is a perceptible quickening of the tempo; the allusions to the 'motto' are taken up with some gusto. As the tempo increases still further, we come across one of Rakhmaninov's weaker passages where all the glitter of the piano-writing cannot wholly disguise the stagnation of the supporting harmony –

eight bars rooted on a repeated B flat in the bass followed by an almost identical seven-bar passage on a G sharp. However, help is at hand when the violas introduce an ingenious new variant of the Second Subject against which Rakhmaninov contrives to fit neat references to the second paragraph of the First Subject. He is not normally credited with such skill in counterpoint as this:

Fig. 50

(The notation here has been changed from sharps to flats to facilitate reading.)

This combination of ideas is extended for some time, with the pianist introducing increasingly martial rhythms which, as the music gathers momentum, turn into a throbbing pattern of repeated chords leading to a great climax as trumpets blare out the 'motto' theme in various forms. A recapitulation of sorts is reached as the full orchestra brings back a majestic version of the original theme, against which the pianist pounds out a massive but immensely stirring treatment of the 'motto' theme. It is an unforgettable moment, a climax which sets the nerves tingling with excitement.

There follows a long rhapsodic extension of the second limb of the original subject which, having climbed to a dramatic peak, gradually subsides in a drawn-out chromatic descent, losing all its recent display of energy as it does so. In a moment of true inspiration Rakhmaninov re-introduces the Second Subject as a horn solo backed by an almost inaudible rustle of strings. It is a perfect evocation of the twilight hour, the tranquillity of which is only briefly disturbed at the soloist's next entry which takes place against piled-up references to the four-note 'motto' theme. In what must be one of the finest passages in the whole concerto, we now find a combination of the 'motto' theme 'augmented' – notes twice as long – against a dreamy version of the Second Subject given to the cellos.

Fig. 51

For several phrases this dialogue continues until a huge spread chord of C *major* marks a significant resting-place. It is the first time that this particular harmony has been heard in the whole movement, and it leads into a drifting improvisational descent in which the rhythms of three-against-five or, if you prefer, six-against-ten, give a beautifully calculated impression of disintegration. Gradually the music sinks lower and lower until, at precisely the moment where it is most needed, a more positive rhythmic impulse is established by the strings. Only the cellos try to sustain the previous mood of nostalgia, but the increasing impetus of the piano part puts a stop to their lament, and the movement ends in a forcefully abrupt manner that firmly stamps out any previous tendency to indulge in self-pity.

The four introductory bars to the slow movement provides a cunning modulation from C minor, the key of the first movement, to E major, the key of the second. It is a very substantial shift of tonality, as a glance at the chart on page 50 will show; E major is an almost total contradiction of every feature of C minor. Despite this, Rakhmaninov had a famous precedent to follow: Beethoven in his Third Piano Concerto exploits an exactly comparable contrast of keys, without even allowing us the luxury of a modulation to smooth the way. Indeed, Beethoven seems possibly to have been in the composer's mind since the opening bars of the piano part bear a slight relationship to the start of the 'Moonlight' Sonata, albeit much romanticised. (A more probable influence is the slow movement of Chopin's Third Piano Sonata, Op. 58, where at one point an uncannily similar passage is to be found.) There is a delightful ambiguity about the rhythm of what, at this stage, is essentially an accompaniment to a sequence of expressive woodwind solos. It is based on the simple mathematical proposition that $4 \times 3 = 3 \times 4$; but does it? While the arithmetical total may indeed be the same, in music there is an obvious difference of stress between ♫♫♫♫ (4 × 3) and  (3 x 4).

What Rakhmaninov does is to blur this distinction so that while the 'pulse' of the music is actually four to the bar, the ear tends to hear it as three:

Fig. 52

The pianist continues with these subtly contrived patterns while first a flute and then a clarinet spell out the hauntingly beautiful tune that is so typical of the composer. Its sadness is tinged with longing, and it is interesting to see quite how this yearning character is achieved. We have already discovered that the seventh note of the scale is called the 'leading' note because it 'leads' the way back to the Tonic, or 'home' note of the scale. Now, if one lingers on this leading note for some time, it creates a positive sense of 'longing' to be allowed to rise to the note above. The third and fourth note of this famous melody is E sharp repeated, which, in this immediate context, is the leading note that 'longs' to be allowed to rise to the F sharp a semitone above, thereby establishing (however briefly) the key of F sharp minor. In the next bar the tune lingers on a D sharp, which, again in this context, is the leading note of E major. In other words, the yearning character of the music is achieved by exploiting the fundamental nature of scales, the notes with the most stress on them always 'longing' to be allowed to rise to the note immediately above.

The tune extends to a considerable length, displaying a characteristic tendency to circle round a few adjacent notes at a time. In due course it is taken over by the piano, not as one might expect with rich additional harmonies, but in the simplest possible form, as if with one finger – though the left hand does lend its support an octave below as the tune develops.

A third version of the theme duly appears in the violins, now in the Dominant key of B major. 'Enough is enough' says the pianist, not allowing them to extend the melody to its full length. With a slight increase in tempo, he introduces a more flowing development based on one fragment of the original theme. A whole sequence of rising patterns, accompanied by poignant sighs in the orchestra leads to the first great climax of the movement which, though brief, makes an unforgettable impact.

Now, we have seen how important a part 'repeats' play in the structure of classical music. Rakhmaninov does not subscribe so slavishly to convention as to have a literal repeat of this section; instead he finds an ingenious and novel way of observing the tradition by repeating it a tone down, in a different key. Furthermore, the rising patterns of which I spoke are increasingly agitated the second time round, sixteen notes to a bar instead of twelve. We still find the same climax though it is even more weightily orchestrated.

With another slight increase in tempo the pianist embarks on a solo passage, in essence a drawn-out rising scale in the right hand with a rippling accompaniment in the left. It reaches its peak on a massive chord of C sharp major, decorated with a whirling flurry of notes that are destined to change the entire character of the movement. With no further warning we are plunged into a miniature scherzo, demanding the most nimble fingers. (It is a plan Rakhmaninov was to develop, though on a rather more elaborate scale, in his Third Concerto.) Although our attention is inevitably drawn towards the brilliant solo part, the orchestral contribution should not be disregarded for it seems to be related to the 'motto' theme from the first movement. I cannot be positive about this, but there is enough of a resemblance to arouse one's suspicions:

Fig. 53

Although the function of this animated section is to be a 'built-in' scherzo, it is extremely brief and is brought to a halt by a huge scale that explodes out of a rumbling trill in the bass. A brief cadenza is calmed by a caressing phrase from two soothing flutes and, sweet release, we arrive at a reprise of the opening melody, its ending gloriously extended by violins accompanied by bell-like chords on the piano. Although the mixture may prove to be too luscious for some palates, there is no denying that the proportions of the movement are beautifully balanced.

In its very much more romanticised way, there is another intriguing link with Beethoven when we reach the start of the third movement. Beethoven's Fourth Concerto has a remarkable slow movement, a dialogue between piano and orchestra in which the orchestra's aggression is gradually tamed by the sheer expressive tenderness of the piano part. At the very end of the movement, the soloist has a cadence that is like a deeply felt sigh of almost unbearable sadness. Then, without warning of so abrupt a change of mood, we hear a distant march, so quiet to begin with that it is heard more as a rhythm than as a tune.

Rakhmaninov uses a similar formula. Like Beethoven, he ends his slow movement with a sigh, but whereas Beethoven's is in E minor and filled with a sense of desolation, Rakhmaninov's is in E major and the sigh is one of utter content. As the luscious final chord dies away, we hear a comparable suggestion of a distant march, even less of a tune than Beethoven's. Here the resemblance ends. Beethoven's finale being a joyous *jeu d'esprit*, while Rakhmaninov's is heroically romantic.

A tiny but significant call to action tends to pass almost unnoticed, so quickly is it swamped by stamping chords from the full orchestra and a glittering cascade of notes from the pianist, but it is worth mentioning since it is a terse reference to the 'motto' theme from the first movement, now in this guise:

Fig. 54

For a moment or two the soloist seems to take over the harpist's role with the sort of sweeping arpeggio figures that one associates with Tchaikovsky's ballet music, but with the return of the orchestra a martial rhythm is established, bringing what has in effect been an introduction to an end. The first main subject of the movement now makes its appearance, heavily cluttered with notes, it is true, but essentially very simple fare.

Fig. 55

(Note that section 2 is identical in pattern to section 1 but a third lower.)

Soloist and orchestra toy with this idea for a little while until it is superseded by a gently floating waltz that is prevented from suggesting a haunted ballroom only by the continued activity of the soloist who is too busily occupied to have much time for ghosts. The music builds to a climax which is topped by an aggressively percussive version of the theme quoted above. With a loudly stamped out A-men the orchestra retires from the fray, leaving the soloist to show for the first time that this idea also has lyrical possibilities. Easing back the tempo and widening the scope of the melody, the piano-part prepares the way for the gracious Second Subject to appear.

By giving it to the violas rather than the violins (it is their turn later), Rakhmaninov suggests that this very operatic melody should be thought of in terms of a tenor aria, thereby establishing a kinship to the 'Love' theme from Tchaikovsky's *Romeo and Juliet* overture which Tchaikovsky actually gave to a tenor in a sketched operatic version. But if the violas are standing in for a tenor hero, the piano becomes the regal heroine he is serenading. Passion flames and then dies. Suddenly and mysteriously the whole mood of the movement changes.

From a purely academic point of view, this truly fascinating section can be regarded as a straightforward if subtle variant of the theme quoted above. Written out at the same pitch, one can easily detect that the second example is a smoothed-out version of the first with the notes packaged in groups of threes.

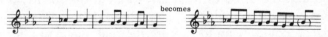

Fig. 56

Not only is the piano writing mysterious in its suggestion of tinkling bells, strangely muffled, but the orchestral part as well is positively eerie, with a subterranean drone above which hollow chords and softly chinking cymbals seem barely to mark the passage of time.

It is my personal conviction, though I have never seen it suggested elsewhere, that this section commemorates in music the sessions of hypnosis that the composer underwent before he could regain enough self-confidence to be able to write this work. If ever sounds could be described as hypnotic, they are these, and the eager vitality with which the piano-part emerges from the state of trance surely symbolises the rebirth of the composer's creative self.

As though he must set to and learn his craft anew, Rakhmaninov dismantles the music and rebuilds it as a brilliantly contrived little fugue. With ever-mounting confidence the music seems to soar on wings, the spirit liberated at last from doubt and despair. It is an interpretation I would not venture to offer were it not for the strange story of Dr Dahl, whose significance Rakhmaninov endorsed with the dedication of the concerto.

However, he was too good a composer to allow the movement to degenerate into a form of autobiography, and all the various elements are assembled into a remarkably satisfactory formal balance. Considering how important a part the traditional cadenza for soloist plays in the First and Third Concertos, Rakhmaninov shows unusual restraint in eliminating all but the merest gestures in that direction in this, his most popular work. The apotheosis of the movement comes with the magisterial reappearance of the Second Subject with the full strings in unison and tremendous throbbing chords from the piano. If the concerto may seem to begin with the tolling of a funeral bell, it certainly ends with the most triumphant peal imaginable.

Soloist and orchestra had been in brilliant form and Keith found the final moments of the concerto an overwhelming experience. The music alone was enough to fire the blood, but when one added to that the sight of those incredibly agile hands as they flew across the keyboard, the electric energy that seemed to emanate from the conductor's baton and the sense of total involvement that nearly a hundred musicians brought to their task, he realised that no recording, however perfect, could begin to capture the real magic of performance. At his side, John was saying something but the tumult of applause was such that he couldn't really hear nor, for the moment, did he feel capable of speech such was the emotional uplift within his usually rather stolid self. A burst of cheering greeted soloist and conductor as they returned to the platform for a third – or was it a fourth? – time, and for a moment Keith's habitual reserve nearly gave way. But then he suddenly felt a little self-conscious about shouting a word as unfamiliar as 'Bravo!' so he contented himself with clapping harder than before.

During the interval John took Keith for a stroll round the building; there was an interesting exhibition of musical portraits that was worth the visit, especially as it included several striking photographs of Bartók.

'I'm a bit worried about the Bartók,' said Keith, a touch of anxiety in his voice. 'I enjoyed the Rakhmaninov so much; I don't want the evening to be spoilt by a lot of horrible noises. Anyway, what does he mean by "Concerto for Orchestra"? Surely there ought to be a soloist?'

John laughed. 'Concertos for Orchestra are actually a very old-fashioned idea; think of Bach's Brandenburg Concertos for instance, or all the works called "Concerto Grosso" by Handel or Vivaldi or Corelli. Bartók's intention was to revive that concept but in completely modern terms. It was written with the Boston Symphony Orchestra in mind. At the time, Bartók was living in America in considerable poverty and Koussevitsky, who was a very great conductor, commissioned him to write the Concerto to provide him with some much-needed cash. Bartók obviously felt it'd be a nice compliment to the orchestra to plan it as a concerto rather than a symphony, so that the individual players would feel they were all being given the status of soloists in their own right. There isn't a dull part in the score; everyone has a chance to show their skills. Maybe it isn't quite the same as standing out in front like a real concerto soloist, but you've got to have a soloist's technique to be able to get round the notes.'

'But won't it be awfully noisy?' protested Keith. 'I mean, I loved the climaxes in the Rakhmaninov because they had such marvellous tunes; there won't be anything to compare with that will there?'

'Oh come off it Keith,' said John. 'Be sensible; the Rakhmaninov was written back in 1900, the Bartók in 1944. You wouldn't expect pictures or novels or sculpture to be remotely the same with a gap of nearly half a century between them; why should music be any different? Art doesn't stand still. Composers are always having to find new ways of saying things that their predecessors said before them. The problem for the present-day artist in any field is that all the easy ways have been used up; it's that much harder to find a personal way of putting your message across. You won't find Rakhmaninov-type tunes in Bartók but that doesn't mean you won't find *any* tunes. There are lots of them, most of them based on popular music.'

Keith grunted in audible disbelief. 'Popular?'

'Yes, genuine music of the people. He spent literally years walking round Hungary and Romania collecting folk-music from its original sources; you could say it entered his blood-stream. When you talk of

Bartók as being "noisy" you do him a terrible injustice; he had the most incredibly acute hearing and was fascinated by the tiny sounds of nature like insects. Some of his music could legitimately be called a Nocturne, though in a quite different way from anything Chopin ever imagined.

'But going back to what I said just now about composers having to find new ways of using sound – you remember the start of Schubert's "Unfinished" Symphony, with those low unison notes on cellos and basses, very quiet, and then that sort of rustling figure in the violins like the murmur of the breeze?'

'That's real music,' said Keith with a note of enthusiasm in his voice. 'That was the first symphony that really got through to me when I was a boy.'

'Well,' said John, 'when the Bartók starts, try to realise that it's basically exactly the same musical conception, cellos and basses playing a very quiet unison followed by a rustling murmur on the violins. Yet the actual *sound* is completely different; in fact I think it's even more magical because it's so mysterious and evocative. Think of it as a film-shot, and the camera takes you through some rusty iron gates up a neglected drive towards one of those pseudo-Gothic monstrosities that people like Boris Karloff always used to be living in, and it's a dark night with a gibbous moon (I'm never quite sure what that means but it sounds good) and then suddenly you get an awful start as a bird flies out of a bush right in front of you.'

During this somewhat unorthodox exposition of Bartók's music, the two men had begun to ascend the shallow flights of stairs that would bring them back to their places in the auditorium. After exchanging a few murmured 'Excuse-me's as they eased past those who had already returned to their row, they sat down, Keith's apprehensions considerably calmed. He took up the programme and noted that there were five movements to be . . . the flow of thought faltered momentarily in his mind as he wondered which word would be the more apt, 'endured' or 'enjoyed'. There was a flurry of excitement to his left as Sally and Terry hurried along the row scattering 'sorry's as they came. It seemed they'd encountered some friends they'd met at a music-camp the previous summer, but any further details were stifled as the leader strode on to the platform. John touched his sleeve.

'Try not to *think* too hard when you're listening to this', he muttered quietly; 'enjoy the sound for its own sake and above all, let it play on your *imagination*. I think you'll find it absolutely stunning; if you don't, the drinks are on me. Ah, here he is . . .' and applause spread like a wave through the hall as the conductor came back on to the platform.

14 _Concerto for ninety_

The _Concerto for Orchestra_ by Béla Bartók (1943–5) is a perfect demonstration of the twentieth-century approach to the art of orchestration. In a century of enormous and rapid changes of style it is obviously impossible to find one definitively representative work since not only does each composer have his personal imprint but the implications of nationalism need to be taken into account as well. French composers such as Debussy and Ravel use orchestral tone-colour in a different way from their English contemporaries Elgar, Holst or Vaughan Williams; an essentially Germanic composer such as Schoenberg produces a different texture from the Austrian Mahler or the Italian Respighi. Stravinsky is something of a special case since he was consciously to eliminate the overtly Russian style of his brilliant early ballets in favour of a more cosmopolitan idiom. However, during the last two decades the boundaries of nationalism have tended to become eroded due to the rapid increase of new electronic methods of sound production. We are in the midst of a revolution in musical sound, yet it is only marginally more radical from that which occurred to the piano between the period of Mozart and Chopin, or to the orchestra between Haydn and Berlioz. Technological change now moves at a faster rate and the modern composer is being provided with an entirely new range of tonal resources more quickly than they can be fully absorbed, but this does not necessarily mean that the orchestra is obsolete. Bartók's Concerto has more than proved its staying powers, and deserves to be claimed as an enduring classic.

To appreciate its qualities to the full we certainly need to be able to respond to its Hungarian accent; we also need to be aware of Bartók's methods of musical construction, in particular his exploitation of patterns based on one chosen interval. For example in the second movement we find a series of tunes played by instruments a sixth apart, a third apart, a seventh apart, a fifth apart, a second apart, and a closing chord which blends all these various intervals into one surprisingly harmonious whole.

The work begins, as has been suggested, with a twentieth-century treatment of a nineteenth-century formula, but whereas Schubert's opening to the 'Unfinished' Symphony tends to move through rather close intervals and, for all its implicit romanticism, to have an essentially classical orderliness about it, Bartók's cellos and basses cover a wider span, while the subsequent shimmer on the strings is designed to give an almost formless impression. In cinematic terms we might compare this to a shot of black water at dawn, moving sluggishly at the lakeside, and then, as the camera pans upwards, a glimpse of reeds rustling their heads as a whiff of breeze sets them dancing. A fluttering figure on a pair of flutes that begins on a single note and then briefly opens outwards suggests a bird stretching its wings after its nocturnal rest. Such images have their value, if only to offer some refuge from the dead hand of the sort of clinical analysis that I call 'musical anatomy'. All the same it is necessary to reiterate that although Bartók willingly admitted that he was inspired by the *sounds* of nature, it is dangerous to assume that his music is equally a *picture* of nature. The creative musical mind is divided between intellect and imagination, biased one way or the other according either to the temperament of the composer or the demands of the composition. When Delius wrote *On hearing the first cuckoo in spring* his prime concern was imaginative; when Beethoven wrote the *Grosse Fuge*, his intellect was the dominant factor.

The Bartók Concerto is a particularly fascinating example of a perfect balance between these two opposing aspects of composition, since while it continually evokes the most imaginative responses, it is in fact a work that is kept under a surprisingly rigid intellectual control. Thus we find areas where one interval or one rhythmic pattern will appear time and again in varied colours, while simultaneously, in a different part of the orchestra a melody of extreme intensity will give an impression of inspired improvisation. As far as the listener is concerned this implicit division between intellect and emotion applies to virtually all but the most lightweight music and is, perhaps more than any other factor, responsible for the lesser or greater popularity of individual works. The more the composition is biased towards the open expression of emotion the more immediate its appeal is likely to be to the untrained ear; hence the enormous popularity of such composers as Rakhmaninov, Tchaikovsky or Chopin. The more a piece is intellectually demanding, the less it is likely to appeal to the unitiated listener. This is not to say that the educated ear cannot also respond to the emotional appeal of music, but rather that to be able to appreciate it at two levels enhances the enjoyment. Nobody can say for sure what is going on in another person's mind as he or she listens to a piece of music; but it is indisputable that a trained musician with ability to absorb the total aural experience at any given moment, as well as to relate it to past events, will be in far closer touch with the composer's intentions than someone who merely enjoys music as a pleasing or stimulating sound.

With this in mind it might be illuminating to listen to the Bartók concerto through the rather different ears of our little group and compare their responses. In the case of Sally and Terry, being performers themselves they mostly identify with the players, more concerned with *how* the sounds are produced and the technical challenges they present than with the actual content of the music. Their sense of vicarious involvement would be much the same were the music to be Rimsky-Korsakov, Debussy, Mahler or Stockhausen; the 'means' offer a greater source of fascination than the 'ends'. Keith and John, however, typify two very different kinds of listener, the one responding almost exclusively to the appeal (or lack of it!) of actual sound, the other very much aware of Bartók's skills as orchestrator, manipulator of material, and (to use a term favoured by Stravinsky) as 'inventor' – the creator of sounds uniquely his own. Let us try to see into their minds as the first movement of this masterpiece of twentieth-century music unfolds. (For those fortunate enough or interested enough to lay their hands on a score I have identified the various sections by bar-numbers.)

KEITH	JOHN
Bars 1–34	He's dead right about this being ghostly; those violins send quite a shiver through you; and the flutes – I see what he meant about the bird suddenly fluttering out of the bush.	What a mixture of imagination and discipline; the form's so clear – unison cellos and bases, and then the *tremolando* widening and narrowing again on violins. He's so clever the way he uses one interval like a fourth to give a them a character of its own.

Fig. 57

Each time it comes he widens the pattern, stretching it further, but you can always feel those fourths controlling the shape.

The first real theme on that solo flute is magic, a tangible shape emerging out of the mist. You can tell he's Hungarian, can't you, with those close angular intervals in the tune, and the four quick notes at the beginning of the bar always tending to halt in mid-movement:

One of the flutes has got a bit of tune now; it *does* sound different, almost oriental. I suppose that's what he meant by the 'Hungarian accent'.

Fig. 58

Bars 35–63

The cellos seem to be stirring things up a bit here. . . .

He's still using patterns based on fourths in the cellos but they're twice as quick now; and he's got the violas imitating them. Lovely wave effect as the lower strings move in contrary motion. Those three trumpets just picking up a subtle suggestion of the flute theme – anyone else would have given that to oboes but the trumpets give it a sort of ritual quality; like priests in some ancient temple moving through a forest of gently swaying dancers.

That bit on the trumpets sounds rather strange; I'd expect something more brilliant from them. Sounds more suitable for oboes I would have thought; it seems too sad for trumpets.

Just listen to those violins divided into four parts; that's Bartók at his most passionate. I like the way he just touched in the most important notes with a spot of woodwind so that the string tone is reinforced but never obscured. And that central horn part makes a marvellously strong

Ah, this is more like it; there's some real passion in those violin parts, and I can see what John meant about Folksong; there's a real touch of the gipsy violins here.

167

KEITH   JOHN

core. The last phrase is fabulous, high up on the G string – makes the music sound so intense.

Bars 63–75   Bit of a five-finger exercise here, but I must say it's very exciting the way he repeats it over and over, whipping up the tempo as he goes.

One simple five-note pattern:

Fig. 59

and he repeats it thirteen times adding to the excitement all the time by bringing in more instruments and increasing the tempo. It's a great way of generating energy, an updated version of what Beethoven does when he breaks into the *allegro* of his Fourth Symphony.

Bars 76–154   It almost seemed as though the music literally snapped apart there, and even I could sense that it was like a new chapter beginning. Funny rhythm though, gives the feeling of tipping the tune forward into the next phrase, almost as though the dancers were stumbling.

Well, that's the introduction over and for all its imaginative impact it's structurally just the same as the introduction Haydn, Mozart or Beethoven so often used at the start of a symphonic movement. And now, when the main part of the movement begins, it springs directly out of the little five-note pattern. The irregular rhythm gives it an extra spice though.

Fig. 60

The mood seems a bit less bouncy here, though I recognise that five-finger exercise; he even turns it

Even here fourths are the most prominent interval, as horns and violins stress with that held-back phrase.

KEITH

JOHN

upside-down. Bet John didn't think I'd spot that.

Fig. 61

Three upward whooshes on the woodwind the five-note pattern again, a little gap and we're away into a sort of development section in which the five-note group plays an important part, both ascending and descending. But then that long climb-down on the flute seems to bring everything almost to a halt, or at any rate a slightly fidgety sit-down on one harmony.

The strings seem to be more lyrical here though I don't quite see where it's all leading to. Oh, it seems to have settled down on one chord for a bit.

Bars 154–230 This is nice, just look at young Terry – he's really imagining himself playing that oboe solo. Doesn't sound too difficult either.

Talk about classical form ... here's a second subject if ever I saw one. Such a simple little tune too, virtually on two notes, just a solo oboe over that gently syncopated accompaniment.

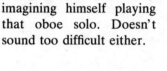

Fig. 62

I like the occasional quiet comment from the harp, and the way the violins and cellos just nudge the rhythm along whenever the tune stands still. Each new version of the tune has a little more activity around it; the colours are brighter too, clarinets with quite a busy harp part, then flutes and oboe widely spaced with that delicate dancing figure in the violins, like snowflakes. And just as you think he'll start to build it

I must say this isn't half as tough as I thought it was going to be. Those fluttering violins are a really pretty effect, and I like the contrast between the low strings and high woodwind.

KEITH | JOHN

One can really hear what's going on.

all up he slows things down, the lower strings putting on the brakes.

Bars 231–48

Whoops! Off we go; that was a surprise. It's the five-finger exercise going mad all over the orchestra.

What a beautifully prepared trap for the listener – almost lulling us to sleep and then whizzing off like that, using the five-note theme as a flail to whip up our attention.

Bars 248–71

The cellos seem to be imitating the violins here; I feel I ought to be able to recognise the tune but I'm not quite sure.

Super counterpoint here, cellos copying the second fiddles a bar later, and then the bassoons shadowing the oboes; and always the fourths giving the themes a sort of family relationship. It's a brilliant way of unifying the whole movement.

Fig. 63

It's getting a bit complicated for me – but there's another of those sudden breaks.

Then just as you think it's all getting a bit academic and predictable he chops it off.

Bars 272–312

Another change of pace; the clarinet's got the tune now so he really does seem to be focussing on different instruments in turn. I can see why he called it a Concerto for Orchestra, and I can feel that all these patterns are related somehow.

Once again he catches us out with a change of tempo and yet another 'fourths-family' tune.

Fig. 64

A nice change of colour when he gives it to the cor anglais, and then later on at half-speed to the bass clarinet. The texture's so beautifully clear, you can hear all the dialogue between the various woodwind instruments. And it all tapers down to a single clarinet playing quite slowly, fourths again . . . another lull before the storm.

Bars 313–96	And now we're away again with another whoosh from that five-finger exercise; at least I can recognise that each time it comes. I say, this is a terrific passage for the brass, trombones, trumpets, horns and tuba, all joining in. . . . Talk about Joshua blowing down the walls of Jericho – what a fantastic climax.

Ah, here comes one of my favourite bits, a tremendous fugue for brass. Naturally the theme is all built on fourths again, but it's such a strong version this time.

Fig. 65

He kicks off with a single trombone then brings another for the second entry; next it's the trumpets, with quite traditional entries of the fugue subject. Then there's a great moment when the horns come in with the theme upside-down, 'inverted'.

Fig. 66

They all have a go at that and then return to the original version, overlapping so tightly that it sounds like an echo chamber. And then there's that fabulous chord for full orchestra that literally seems to burst apart.

Bars 396–475	Phew! That was tremendous. And now I actually recognise the tune I said

And what happens next? A complete change of mood back to the gentle tranquillity of that little

171

KEITH	JOHN
Terry would enjoy, the one on the oboe all round two notes. Oh, it's a clarinet this time, but I must say, a lot of the landmarks are surprisingly clear. There's that dancing violins bit, and he's slowing down again. I think I know what to expect now; it means that just when everything seems quiet he'll go shooting off again.	two-note tune that I called the second subject, only this time it's on a clarinet. He extends it in a very similar way, a sort of recapitulation really. It's near enough the same to serve a useful structural purpose, but there are lots of subtly different touches in the orchestration. I like the way he quietens it all down again before the final explosive reappearance of the true First subject from which so many derivations have sprung.

	KEITH	JOHN
Bars 476–514	Yes, I was right, mounting tension and then all the strings belting out a theme I'm sure I've heard before. I get the feeling he's heading for the finish.	And here we go into the Recapitulation of the First Subject, pretty unmistakable with all the strings belting it out in unison.

Fig. 67

But it isn't a true recapitulation as it's far too short for that; more of a reminder really.

	KEITH	JOHN
Bars 514–End	There's that brass theme again; impressive isn't it. Goodness me, it's ended.	What a stroke of genius after all those swift ascending scale fragments to impose such authority with the subject of the brass figure, and then the five-note theme upside-down just to put the lid on it.

To his surprise Keith has actually understood much more of the music than he expected to. Partly this is due to the clarity of the structure, much of which is built on traditional lines; but although there would appear to be rather a large number of different themes in terms of conventional analysis, the 'family relationship' established through the recurring use of the interval of a fourth does register with the listener, even though he may not be able to pinpoint precisely why the themes seem alike. On reflection he may feel cheated that the passionate 'gipsy' theme from the introduction failed to reappear, but here again, Bartók is following classical precedents. For example, Beethoven's second Symphony has a substantial introduction that is both beautiful and profound, but no significant reference is made to it in the ensuing *Allegro*. In fact Bartók's introduction is extremely relevant to the main movement since from the very start it establishes the importance of the fourth as the interval from which virtually everything springs. Even what I have referred to as the five-finger exercise is what might be termed a 'stretched' fourth.

Keith was quite looking forward to the second movement. In conversation John had referred to it as 'Noah's Ark', and had reminded him of the old song about 'The animals went in two by two, Hurrah! Hurrah!' Whether Bartók had ever contemplated any relationship between this movement and the legend of Noah is open to doubt, but the idea fits the music so admirably that it at least serves to imprint its most notable feature on the memory. Certainly the plan of the movement proves to be a particularly apt justification for the title 'Concerto for Orchestra', since bassoons, oboes, clarinets, flutes and trumpets in turn are put into the spotlight, each time in pairs. (Bartók actually called the movement *'Giuoco delle coppie,'* 'A game of couples.')

As an interesting sidelight on the ease with which erroneous traditions can be established, many recordings of this work give a false impression of the second movement, since the metronome mark in the published score was incorrectly shown as 74 beats to the minute instead of the 94 in Bartók's manuscript, a fairly substantial difference of tempo. Although the slower tempo can be quite attractive in its slightly pawky way, it doesn't show off the virtuosity of the players in the manner which Bartók presumably intended.

A not too obtrusive side-drum sets the rhythm tapping on its way, and then the first couple 'take the floor'. They are bassoons, moving in exact parallel a sixth apart. The tone is jocular, even a little rustic, the accompaniment minimal. In due course two oboes take over; like the bassoons, they move in parallel but a third apart. Their material is distinctly fussier in character, and it is easy enough to imagine the bassoons as a pair of old men sharing reminiscences, while the oboes are a couple of housewives engaged in slightly shrewish gossip. It is enough at least to cause a bit of a stir in the lower strings before the next couple make their appearance. This time it is the clarinets, rather less euphonious than their predecessors since they are spaced a seventh apart, sevenths inevitably tending to sound like very out of tune octaves to the uninitiated ear. Next in line come the flutes, adding a faintly Chinese flavour with their parallel fifths. It is worth mentioning that towards the end of this little duet they do momentarily take independent paths, albeit only in a rather discreet and barely noticeable way.

As the movement progresses the strings seem to take an increasing interest in what is going on, and after each wind duet the lower strings in particular tend to make some active comment. The paired trumpets, a discordant second apart, evoke a positively shuddering reaction from the violins, possibly a sarcastic reaction on Bartók's part against the withering criticism he had so often received from the academic establishments of many countries. The side-drum, silent since its introductory solo, calls a halt to the proceedings with a peremptory rhythm; the mood changes as trumpets, trombones and tuba introduce a smoothly intoned chorale, whose air of piety must be regarded as suspect in this context, the more so since the side-drum keeps making fidgety interjections whenever the brass theme comes to rest. As interludes go it's on the brief side, and the oboe and flute in turn soon display an irreverent desire to return to more frivolous matters.

And so it is that we return to the original material, although characteristically Bartók avoids slavish repetition while acknowledging the structural value of a reprise. For instance we now find *three* bassoons instead of two; the oboes and clarinets form a garrulous quartet instead of politely taking turns; then flutes, clarinets and bassoons all pitch in together. As for the trumpets, they appear to march through a haunted house with much shuddering in the strings and spine-tingling *glissandi* from the harps. Suddenly all movement freezes on a single chord; with a show of impatience the woodwind repeat it a number of times before freezing into immobility once more. A few taps on the side drum end this highly original and unusual movement.

Before we leave it, it is worth while to take a more inquiring look at the closing harmony. Bartók has been at considerable pains to establish certain fixed intervals between the instruments comprising each 'couple'. These intervals are given a final seal of approval by being ingeniously combined in the 'freeze' chord which concludes the movement. To make the picture clearer I have shown them separately below and in the order in which they appear, but in the music proper, all are sounded simultaneously.

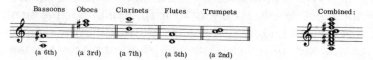

Fig. 68

The third movement, to which Bartók gave the title 'Elegia' or Elegy is the most magically scored of the five. Besides serving the traditional function of a slow movement, it helps to unify the Concerto by referring back to fragments from the opening introduction. For example it again employs the fourth as the most significant interval, as the opening bars clearly show, whether in the basses:

Fig. 69

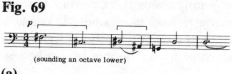

(a)

the answering cellos:

(b)

the violas that follow a bar later:

(c)

or the ensuing second violins:

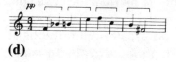

(d)

175

The similarity of the patterns is evident even to the untrained eye (or ear!), and the unfolding of such shapes so that they are closely interwoven is a favourite technique of Bartók's that is particularly apparent in this movement. Soon clarinet and flute begin to exchange a fluid rippling figure which might equally well represent a spurt of water from a small fountain or the call of some exotic jungle-bird. No other instruments could produce this particular effect with so liquid a quality, while a gentle glissando on the harp emphasises the suggestion of flowing water. On the other hand, a series of isolated notes on a solo piccolo are equally suggestive of a bird or insect, and the movement in its early stages could certainly be described as a Nocturne without fear of misrepresentation.

After no fewer than eighteen repetitions of the 'ripple', its exact shape is taken up in slow motion and shared in a complex web between six instruments, three flutes and three clarinets each overlapping its neighbour. Violins attempt somewhat abortively to pick up the same pattern but fail to get very far with it; this is hardly surprising since for them much more exciting things lie ahead. Without warning, they launch into an impassioned lament whose wild cry is punctuated by dramatically swooping scales and awesome thumps from the timpani supported by harps and trombones. It needs a retentive memory to recognise this as a violently emotional extension of the very first flute solo in the whole work, the one I described as 'emerging from the mist'.

Original version: bars 30 – 33 of First Movement.

'Reincarnation': bars 34 – 38 of Third Movement.

Fig. 70

Notice that this is not a simple repetition of the original idea though the relationship between the two is far more than mere coincidence. What I have called the Reincarnation has far greater intensity than the fragile flute solo that first caught our attention, partly because of its scoring but also because of the extra beat at the end of the bar, heightening the tension by extending the main notes beyond their expected duration.

This whole section forms an unexpectedly dramatic centrepiece to a movement that starts in the style of a nocturnal impression. An agitated figure that churns around immediately adjacent notes leads to an emphatic theme for all the woodwind in unison, similarly reinforced by explosive blows from brass, timpani and strings. Suddenly, and the effect is the more dramatic for being unheralded, the passionate 'gipsy' theme that was played by divided violins in the initial introduction to the work (bars 51–62, see p. 167) reappears, this time with the full participation of the woodwind. It achieves a stupendous climax, the emotional highspot of the entire concerto; just as the intensity becomes almost unbearable, two 'ripples' from the clarinet and flute remind us of how the movement began. The lower strings, in unison, quietly re-introduce the fundamental pattern of fourths:

Fig. 71

The 'ripples' begin again, elaborated in texture by the addition of second flutes and second clarinets as though the surface of the water were slightly more agitated. (Not surprisingly after the immediately preceding events. . . .) With great calmness, the first violins spell out the simplest of all versions of the 'fourths' theme and the movement dies away to nothing.

The relationship between this central movement and the mysterious and evocative introduction to the first movement is a brilliant piece of planning, underlining, despite the intensely imaginative nature of the music, Bartók's preoccupation with form in the symphonic sense. The bridge between the introduction and the third movement shows his concern for form as a large-scale conception, while the limitation to such 'family' groups as a number of themes based on a similar interval or rhythmic pattern reveals his determination to maintain a positively classical discipline within a work which, by its nature, ran the risk of being a loosely constructed series of showcases for different sections of the orchestra.

The fourth movement has as its subtitle '*Intermezzo Interrotto*', or 'Interrupted Intermezzo'; although it might be described as a scherzo in spirit, the 'joke' aspect is not revealed until later. After its initial four notes on unison strings, which are distinctly menacing in tone, the mood changes abruptly as a solo oboe introduces a folk-like tune with an instant appeal, despite its asymmetrical rhythms.

Fig. 72

Although this appears to be completely new it is perhaps worth considering a possible relationship between it and one of the most important elements from the first movement, what Keith thought of as the 'five-finger exercise'. To make the comparison simpler, let us put that much-used fragment into the same area that the oboe tune above occupies.

Fig. 73

The first, second and fifth notes of this fiery little group correspond exactly with the first, second and third notes of the oboe tune. Bartók persists with this new three-note pattern a number of times, just as he persisted with the more aggressive five-note pattern in the first movement. Surely this is yet another example of the 'family relationship' method of unifying a large-scale work, the oboe theme being (as it were) a mild mannered grandchild of its fierce progenitor. The tune is immediately repeated but with a considerable change of tone colour; a clarinet takes over from the oboe, supported, unusually, an octave *lower* by a flute; meanwhile a bassoon provides a mirror image of the melody, duplicating almost exactly its every twist and turn, though with the slight distortions that one might expect from a reflection seen in still but not stagnant water.

For some time Bartók toys with this innocent little melody keeping the accompaniment virtually static, just quietly sustained chords on the strings. Although the music has a certain fey charm it is also a trifle wan, the instruction always being to play quietly. Suddenly the violas produce a tune of remarkable richness, accompanied by bardic chords on the harp. Here is the full-blooded warmth that up to now has been repressed, and a fine contrast it makes to what has gone before.

Fig. 74

Were it not for the slightly angular intervals this might almost be mistaken for Vaughan Williams, so immediate is its lyrical appeal. It is ironic that those critics who earlier in his career had castigated Bartók for his excessive dissonance and ruthless lack of sentiment regarded such unashamed lyricism as a betrayal of his true self, a concession to popular appeal unworthy of so individual an artist. While it is true that the Concerto for Orchestra and the Third Piano Concerto are two of his most immediately approachable and popular works, this does not necessarily mean (as some critics maintain) a decline in his powers but rather the mellowing that comes with recognition too long delayed.

After the violins have appropriated the violas' tune for themselves, the initial little oboe tune returns giving us every justification to believe that the music will continue according to classical precedent. It is at just such moments that great composers take most delight in catching their listeners by surprise, and a surprise there certainly is. A solo clarinet, accompanied in a deliberately trivial style by the strings, produces a tune of unexpected banality based on a descending scale. It is one of the very few examples in the history of music of one composer lampooning another in such a way as to excite open ridicule. This is not the type of affectionate satire that we find in such works as Walton's *Façade* or Ravel's *L'enfant et les Sortilèges*.

It has far more venom in it than that, as the raucous 'raspberry' with which the tune is greeted by the rest of the orchestra clearly shows. The subject of Bartók's malice was the main theme of Shostakovich's 'Leningrad' Symphony, music which he found ludicrously inadequate for the expression of genuine heroism and which he promptly decided to burlesque after a single hearing. Since most audiences today will seldom if ever have heard the Shostakovich work, the joke has rather lost its point; but the humour, barbed though it may be, is still apparent, both in the obvious rude gestures and the musical representation of peals of laughter. It is this section that 'interrupts' the Intermezzo as the title of the movement implies, and the subsequent return of the elegiac viola tune only serves to underline the superiority of Bartók's inspiration. The movement ends quietly with a few gentle references to the naive little tune with which it began.

The Finale might be described as a glorification of the gipsy violinist. A rousing fanfare from the horns causes us to sit up abruptly after the quiet and unostentatious ending to the preceding movement. Then comes an exciting strumming from the lower strings, moving into a breathlessly swift tempo. Second violins set off on a sort of perpetual motion figure in which they are soon joined by their neighbours, the firsts. Once again we find Bartók exploiting the idea of 'family resemblance'; the 'five-finger exercise' theme from the first movement

Fig. 75

proves to be the starting-point for a hectic sprint that continues unbroken for 294 notes!

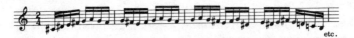

Fig. 76

The sheer energy of the music sweeps the audience along in its wake; never is the title Concerto for Orchestra more aptly justified than in this movement where, amongst the violins in particular, there can be no passengers.

At a point where hysteria nearly breaks in Bartók restores a touch of symphonic respectability to the proceedings with a brief attempt at a fugue, bravely initiated (though it must be admitted without much success) by the second bassoon. A few woodwind colleagues follow his lead; indeed a solo flute even tries to introduce a note of gentility by inverting the fugue subject and slowing it down. However, this brief interlude is little more than an opportunity for the string players to wipe the sweat off their brows and pull the odd broken hairs from their bows, for in less than a minute they are off again at as wild a pace as ever, the essentially rustic quality of the music underlined by the bagpipe-like drone in the bass.

But now we reach the moment where Bartók shows true greatness as a composer . 'Gipsy Fiddler' pieces have been written by the hundreds, mostly of little musical worth; had Bartók confined this finale to such material alone we might indeed justly complain of a falling-off of inspiration. Instead he plays a trump-card by intro-ducing a magnificent fugal theme on a solo trumpet which strides majestically through the swirling figuration on the strings.

Fig. 77

The first trumpet immediately shows us what this theme sounds like turned upside down; a compressed version follows with horns taking the downward version, second trumpet swiftly overlapping them with the mirror image. Meanwhile the strings continue their dervish dance utterly disregarding the more serious matters which increasingly preoccupy brass and wind. Suddenly all movement is arrested by three abrupt chords for full orchestra and a roll on the timpani.

The tempo eases back somewhat. And now the strings, tentatively at first but with ever-growing confidence, take up the trumpet's fugue. In due course it is the woodwinds' turn to do the same. If one conceives the dance as a physical mode of expression and the fugue as an intellectual one, this entire central section may be seen as a deliberate assertion of the intellect over the body; yet such is the vigour of the actual subject matter that one does not feel let down.

More than 180 bars after the first appearance of that fugue subject, the gipsy element reasserts itself, the physical excitement of the music now intensified by the rapidly throbbing beat of timpani. A little later on there is one more brief easing-up of the tempo before the final dash begins. A swirling pattern in the strings sweeps through widen-ing circles preparing us for a spectacular climax whose precise nature we cannot predict but for which our anticipation is brilliantly aroused. A moment's silence, the musical equivalent of a collective gasp from the audience, and the climax materialises. With immense grandeur, the full brass proclaim a much broadened version of the fugue, while the surrounding scale passages on strings and wind suggest the triumphant waving of multi-coloured banners. (For an almost 'classical' equivalent to this splendid moment turn to the closing pages of the Brahms-Haydn 'St Antoni' Variations; the substance is the same, the idiom completely different.) The final rounding off of the movement after this magnificent passage caused Bartók some difficulty, and the score actually shows two alternative endings, the second of which is the more brilliant. Either way, the work cannot fail since even the most prejudiced audience must respond to the magical beauty of the orchestration in the quiet passages and the sheer physical excitement of the rest. Nevertheless it is worth stressing that a concert performance will always make a more enduring impression than any recording, however perfect. The athletic involvement of the players is a positive contribution to one's enjoyment; to perform any work as challenging as this demands not just virtuosity but a remarkable degree of teamwork, nearly a hundred players working and thinking as one. Even the uninitiated listener will sense this; the sight of all those bows flashing at speed in the finale, the shining brass upraised in glorious waves of sound, the blur of timpani sticks conjuring a thunderous roar from those great copper bowls, all these aspects of music are not to be denied as important contributory factors which neither record, radio nor even television screen can adequately convey.

As John had rightly predicted, Keith was overwhelmed by the experience. The applause was deafening as, at the conductor's behest, the orchestra stood, aware that they had risen to the occasion and met their own exacting standards.

'I wish they'd play that whole last movement as an encore' shouted Keith, and then, shaking his head as though in disbelief, he muttered 'Fantastic' to himself, 'Absolutely fantastic.'

Later, as they made their way down the thronged staircase, he turned to John saying, 'You know, I just can't think how a man can imagine all those sounds and get them all down on paper. You'd think he'd have to have a private orchestra at the ready so that he could try things out. It's amazing that the human brain can visualise sound of that complexity. . . .'

'Well, that's what composition's about,' said John; 'the cultivation of the inner ear. Mind you the electronic composers of today do have exactly what you suggest. The synthesiser is a "private orchestra" on which you can try out all your effects, but somehow it isn't the same. One feels the machine is doing the work as much as the man. Anyway, there's not much excitement in watching a synthesiser playing; I think I'd rather see an orchestra any day. Incidentally did you notice that second harpist, the one with the long blonde hair – I thought she was a bit of alright. Perhaps she'd come and play a concerto with the school orchestra. . . .' With which base thought he led the way towards the car-park.

On the journey back through South London Keith tried not to be distracted by the excited chatter of the youngsters in the back. He wanted to savour the memory of both sight and sound. The Bartók was not familiar enough for him to be able to recall anything but general impressions, but he was well aware how stirred he had been by the sheer impact of the music. Nor did he want to forget the Rakhmaninov, so different in its appeal, and yet even more direct in its assault on his emotions. The concert, he felt, had been a significant milestone in the development of his recently discovered addiction to music and one which he was eager to follow up. It seemed that a lot had happened since he had first, somewhat reluctantly, taken his young nephew Jeremy to the school orchestral rehearsal. Meantime, when he had a few minutes to spare, he was trying to work at his sight-reading as he genuinely wanted to pass the audition to join the choir. He was not to know that destiny had rather different plans for him.

15 __Letter from a friend _____

St. Christopher's
Sydenham
S.E. 26

27th July

My dear Keith

I suppose I should first congratulate you on being appointed manager of your firm's new venture in Carmarthen. Lord knows they want all the new enterprises they can get in that part of the world and you'll not lack applicants for jobs. All the same I can't help feeling really sorry that our joint journey along the pathway to music should be forcibly terminated in this way. It's been a real pleasure to introduce you to so many new experiences and I'm sure you feel that they've enriched your life already. You realise of course that music is a very complex art; that lesson that Tim gave you was still very rudimentary – comparable to 'the cat sat on the mat' in terms of language. But there are quite a number of books of the 'Teach Yourself' kind that will take you a good few steps further; better still, try and find a course at an evening institute or go to one of the many summer schools that offer all sorts of musical opportunities to people like yourself who genuinely want to get to know more about music.

Obviously you're going to a part of the world where concerts like our Festival Hall trip will be difficult to duplicate; but there must, I'm sure, be a local choral society, and if you can renew your involvement with a youth orchestra, preferably at county level, so much the better. As I've always maintained, rehearsals are so much more instructive than concerts, and a lot more fun too. By the way, did you see that Brendel master-class on the box the other night? I know you're not a pianist but I found it absolutely riveting. Things like that really teach you to appreciate the finer points. Incidentally, if there's a local music club, do join it and support it. There's often a sort of snobbish feeling out in the wilds that if young Mr So-and-so is coming all the way to play to *us* he can't be much good. But nowadays standards are so high that there are dozens of young Mr and Miss So-and-so's doing the rounds of small music clubs and playing every bit as well as if they were at the Wigmore Hall.

As you will be making your way on your own I thought it might be helpful to make a list of works you should get to know on record or cassette. I'm sure that company car you'll be driving around will have a decent sound system in it, even though the Welsh hills may blot out Radio 3. It's difficult to know where to begin, the choice is so vast. What I've done is to divide the music up into categories; that way you can pick and choose for yourself. I'll begin with orchestral music, since that's how we first met. You may be a little surprised that I'm going to start with the twentieth-century and work backwards, but I felt that the Bartók made such a tremendous impression on you that it wouldn't be a bad place to start from. You see, so much of the music of our century is immensely colourful and descriptive, and I think at your stage it helps a lot to be able to listen imaginatively rather than intellectually. Anyway, here goes— even if I do feel a bit like a tipster marking your card!

HOLST	*The Planets*	Brilliantly orchestrated but straightforward listening; has some good rousing tunes in it as well as some very evocative 'outer space' effects.
STRAVINSKY	*Petrushka*	As long as you have a clear picture in your mind of what's happening in the ballet, which a good sleeve-note should tell you, this is one of the most vividly descriptive works ever written.
	Pulcinella	Very different; eighteenth-century dances with the added spice of scrunchy harmonies and virtuoso orchestration. There's a duet for trombone and double-bass that is real slapstick comedy.
	Le Baiser de la Fée	Based on Tchaikovsky themes; lots of charm though it lacks the clear story-line of *Petrushka*.
ELGAR	*Cockaigne Overture*	Very descriptive music where again a good programme note will help you.
	Enigma Variations	Don't worry too much about 'who' each variation is; just enjoy the music.

RESPIGHI	*Fountains of Rome* *Pines of Rome* *Roman Festival*	Perhaps not great music, but exhilarating listening and full of vivid imagery.
DEBUSSY	*Prélude à l'après- midi d'un faune* *Images* *La Mer*	I've graded these in difficulty but the more you listen the more they'll grow on you.
MANUEL DA FALLA	*Dances from The Three-Cornered Hat*	Spanish dances with subtle rhythms and a lot of exotic colour. Irrestible.
BRITTEN	*Variations on a theme of Purcell* (originally 'A Young Person's Guide to the Orchestra')	Well, you're not too old to benefit, and it's a great way to learn your different instrumental families.

Obviously I've left a lot out here, Richard Strauss for instance; wonderful music of course but I think you might get a bit lost in the symphonic poems; they're very episodic and you need a guiding hand. Nor have I bothered with short-and-easies like Elgar's *Pomp and Circumstance*, Walton's *Crown Imperial* and so on. You can manage those on your own. So let's turn back into the nineteenth century, now, where the choice is overwhelming. You could well start with a list of overtures, and who better to begin with than Wagner?

WAGNER	Overtures to *Tannhauser* *Lohengrin* *The Flying Dutchman* *The Mastersingers*	All superb, all different. *The Mastersingers* has a wonderful bit near the end where he combines all the tunes, but it needs a good ear to disentangle them.
HUMPERDINCK	*Hansel and Gretel*	A childhood favourite that never loses its appeal; full of tunes, and notable for beautiful writing for horns.
DUKAS	*The Sorcerer's Apprentice*	A marvellously told narrative in music.
TCHAIKOVSKY	*Romeo and Juliet*	A slow starter, but superb once it gets going. Very dramatic.
MENDELSSOHN	Overtures: *A Midsummer Night's Dream* *The Hebrides*	A staggering feat for a teenage composer. Glorious scene-painting.

BERLIOZ   *Carnaval Romain*   Not as much of an orgy as the title suggests, but well worth exploring.

I'm leaving out Beethoven and his predecessors as you'll find your own way to them in time; let's turn to symphonies, and here I think we do have to start at the other end since it is essentially a classical form. The obvious person to begin with is Haydn, but since he wrote 104 it's very much a matter of personal preference. I should go for the late ones rather than the earlier. The nicknames are designed to help people with a bad head for figures. . . .

HAYDN	Symphonies	No. 88 in G	'Letter V'
		No. 92	'Oxford'
		No. 96	
		No. 99	
		No. 100	'The Military'
		No. 101	'The Clock'
		No. 103	'The Drum-roll'
		No. 104	'The London'

As for Mozart, a particular love of mine is No. 29 in A, but the last trilogy, Nos. 39, 40 and 41, represents one of the most amazing feats in musical history since he is supposed to have written all three within the space of six weeks.

Once we come to Beethoven I think it might be helpful to suggest an order in which to tackle them. By all means begin with No. 5 as it has become so familiar; after that I should go to No. 1 for its wonderfully witty finale, No. 2 for its marvellously beautiful slow movement, No. 4 for its mysterious introduction and general good humour, No. 8 for its sizzling finale, No. 7 for its slow movement, No. 6 for its scene painting; leave Nos. 3 and 9 till last as they are far and away the most demanding.

Berlioz's *Fantastic Symphony* is a *must*; it has a wonderfully romantic story behind it which you should read up in his *Memoirs* – quite the most entertaining autobiography ever written by a musician – and the way he uses the orchestra is quite unbelievable considering that it was written only a few years after Beethoven's death.

I don't think I need mention Schubert's 'Unfinished', it's so well-known. But don't neglect the Fifth, which is sheer enchantment all the way.

Once we come to Tchaikovsky the obvious choices must be 5, 4 and 6 in that order, but do realise that his conception of a Symphony is very different from Beethoven's, much more loosely constructed, much more open in its expression of emotion.

Two lightweights I should mention which will give you a lot of pleasure, Mendelssohn's Fourth, 'The Italian', and the Bizet Symphony in C, another precocious work written in his 'teens and not performed until 1935, eighty years after he'd written it! As for Brahms, I should try No. 2 first and then No. 4. Save the others for later. . . .

I'm not sure what to advise you about Bruckner and Mahler; they're very much a matter of personal taste. You may well fall for them, but I warn you they have a very self-indulgent time-span and you must be prepared to listen to individual movements that may last as long as a complete symphony by Mozart or Haydn. If you want a big romantic symphony that is less demanding I'd go for Sibelius's First. I call it Tchaikovsky's Seventh, and I think you'll see why if you listen to it. It's certainly got some tremendous tunes, and a very exciting scherzo.

Well, that lot should keep you going for a year or two so let's go over to concertos now; here the list need not be quite so vast.

I know you enjoyed Rakhmaninov's Second at our Festival Hall concert, but the Third is full of good things, while the First, extensively revised from a student work, is the most compact. It's quite unfairly neglected, largely because the last movement needs a lot of rehearsal. As for the *Rhapsody on a theme by Paganini*, it's a marvellously contrived set of variations, not really a Rhapsody at all.

I think you'd enjoy Prokofiev's Third Piano Concerto for its tremendous vitality, and, in a very different vein, Shostakovich's Second, which he wrote for his son Maxim. Otherwise I think it's back to the nineteenth century where you can hardly go wrong with Schumann, Chopin (No. 2), Liszt (No. 1), Tchaikovsky (No. 1), and in due course both the Brahms and of course all the Beethoven. As for Mozart – well, to me there are at least half a dozen that are perfection, but at this stage you may hanker after a bit more blood and thunder. After all, the concerto is by its very nature a heroic medium.

If I've concentrated on piano concertos it's because they are more immediately popular, but you must widen your horizon to include such delights as the violin concertos of Brahms, Beethoven and Mendelssohn (Elgar comes a little later on) and the cello concertos of Dvořák and Elgar, not to mention the *Variations on a Rococo Theme* by Tchaikovsky which are very beguiling, even if not a full-scale concerto.

Turning now to chamber music, you'll remember that evening when we listened to the Mozart Clarinet Quintet in A and the Schubert Quintet in C. Add the Brahms Clarinet Quintet to the Mozart – again very different in idiom and conception, but especially notable for its slow movement. It literally sounds as though the clarinettist is improvising, pouring out his heart in a profound expression of emotion. For the most immediately captivating example of a piano quintet – need I say a piano plus a string quartet – I would strongly recommend the Schumann; it's a wonderfully virile work, packed with memorable tunes. If, though, you want to believe in miracles, you simply must explore the Mendelssohn Octet (in effect a double string quartet) written when he was sixteen and a work which one can literally describe as flawless.

As to string quartets, Beethoven is the acknowledged master, though I should warn you that he makes demands on his listeners. I should begin with what is known as the first of the Razumovsky Quartets, so called after the patron who commissioned them. Its opus number is 59 No. 1. Do realise, though, that once you begin to move into these more specialised areas, some guidance is not to be scorned. Try to find a sympathetic string player in the locality, perhaps a music student from one of the colleges, who will spare an evening to go through a quartet with you, steering you through the score as you listen to a recording together. Music is a highly specialised language in which the composer is more fluent than ordinary mortals, and there are times when an 'interpreter' can be really helpful.

I hope you can manage to get into a choir or choral society; slogging through the notes of an unfamiliar work may seem heavy going at times but the rewards of performance are deeply satisfying, and what is a truly great experience is to combine with other choirs in one of the choral masterworks like the Verdi Requiem or Elgar's *The Dream of Gerontius*. I promise you you'll never forget such a day. Watching the children in my orchestra at work has shown you what a genuine thrill they get as all the strands begin to come together; even though you may never play an instrument you will be able to experience that thrill yourself in a choral society especially if there's a good conductor in charge.

This letter seems to have become positively Bruckner-like in scale and I still have some O-level tests to mark. I don't know if the exams really teach them the value of music, but at least it means I can give it time in the school syllabus. It seems tragic that so much of our musical activity has to take place out of school hours, when I believe it's one of the most enriching things that life has to offer. You, my friend, have just begun to discover that; believe me, it is not too late. You have an infinite voyage of discovery ahead; take advantage of it, for music was never so accessible as it is today.

Keep in touch and let me know how you get on.

Sincerely,

John Roberts.

Index

Index